Advance Praise for *YE*

"I find your book **absolut** journey of a pioneering woman unafraid of public scrutiny and [with] a determination to tell the truth. **This book must be read by all people who care about the future of the planet and their children."**
— **Dr. Helen Caldicott**, Nobel Peace Prize nominee

"**Excellent**! Easy reading, breezy, personal, interesting, very well-written – and highly informative. **I find the content impeccable.**"
– **Karl Grossman**, Award-winning investigative reporter and environmental journalist, author *COVER UP: What you ARE NOT SUPPOSED to KNOW ABOUT NUCLEAR POWER.*

Praise for *Nuclear Hotseat*

"Libbe HaLevy is the foremost journalist in the country reporting on nuclear power."
– Lauren Steiner, Producer/Host, *The Robust Opposition*

"Your work, as always, continues to be great."
– Harvey Wasserman, Journalist, Author, Host, *Solartopia*

"Thanks for all you are doing and getting the word out. I was in tears listening to your closing remarks."
– Diane Turco, Director, Cape Downwinders

"I live near Indian Point, traveled in Europe during the time of the spiked radiation readings, and travel to Japan for work a few times per year. Your reporting is important to me at home and on the road."
– Listener Daniel

"Goosebumps. *Nuclear Hotseat* gives me goosebumps."
– Listener Jim Torson

YES, I GLOW IN THE DARK!

ONE MILE FROM THREE MILE ISLAND TO FUKUSHIMA AND *NUCLEAR HOTSEAT*

by
LIBBE HALEVY

DEDICATION

To all your children…
and all their children…
and theirs…

"CLOSE ALL YOUR DOORS AND WINDOWS
AND STAY AWAY FROM THEM. STAY INSIDE
AND DO NOT LEAVE YOUR HOMES
UNLESS IT IS ABSOLUTELY NECESSARY."

This was not the vacation I had intended.

Not a drill, not a false alarm. This was really happening. A nuclear reactor malfunctioning only one mile away. An atomic bomb without the fireball... or could it explode? Might it do so? If so, when? Now? Maybe now? No, now? Or now…?

And what if I was already exposed to so much radiation, this very second, and not *just* this very second but constantly, a non-stop x-ray of my entire body, radiation soaking me, saturating me, attacking me from the inside out, the inevitable cancer rot of my cells down to my DNA –

Is this going to kill me?

Am I already dead?

Was it now? Would it happen now? Now??? NOW?????

Everything I'd been raised and trained to be afraid of as coming from the Russians was primed, locked, and loaded,

i

on the ground only one mile away, courtesy my own government.

It had been happening for three days and I didn't bother to pay attention. And now it's too late, isn't it. Is it? Already? Too late???

* * *

This is the story of what happens when someone who is just a person – no privileged standing in the world, no family fortune, old school ties, corporate or political connections to call upon – finds herself caught next to something that we were told could never happen: a malfunctioning, radiation-leaking, out-of-control nuclear reactor.

To be clear, I am not a scientist, engineer, doctor, mathematician, or any kind of technical "expert" to explain the complex nature of subatomic particles, so what follows is not a technical discourse. Rather, it's a subjective telling of the nuclear industry's invisible impact on one life, based upon what I lived through and learned as a result of having been at Three Mile Island.

I share honestly about my personal life so you get to know the human being behind the experience because, as the olde feminist saying goes: "The personal is the political." That's what usually gets ignored, the human side of a nuclear "Oops!" But it's a mistake to separate the human element from the damage the nuclear industry does, especially when things go wrong.

So I invite you to follow this trail of breadcrumbs through my personal journey, one that started with the above-mentioned loudspeaker announcement and hasn't ended yet. I offer it in the hope that you will enjoy the read, perhaps surprise yourself by laughing (it's allowed), and along the way consider a different perspective on nuclear energy. Maybe by the end you'll be willing to take a bit of action, and I provide some guidance as to how to accomplish that as well.

Whatever it is that speaks to you in what follows, may it provide clarity, perspective, and food for thought, or at least a diversion from whatever troubles you in the rest of your life.

Libbe HaLevy
July 16, 2018
Los Angeles, California

CONTENTS

CHAPTER 1

BEFORE

I have never lived in a world that did not have nuclear weapons and the threat of planetary annihilation hanging over us all.

I was the third child of a middle-class couple, born long enough after my siblings to wonder exactly what transpired between my parents on New Year's Eve 1948-49, nine months before my birth. Raised on Chicago's north side with the birth name Loretta Lotman, I attended public schools that provided a remarkably evolved education, including civics classes where we studied the U.S. Constitution and English classes that taught the proper use of apostrophes.

Nuclear information permeated my childhood like a low grade fever. The dropping of the atomic bombs on Hiroshima and Nagasaki at the end of World War II signaled the start of the nuclear age, which insinuated its way into everyone's consciousness.

Ten-thirty every Tuesday morning, the air raid sirens wailed. I knew they were meant to warn us, but I wasn't certain of what. I have only one memory of an actual duck-and-cover exercise in first grade, 1956. I had no idea why we were suddenly crouching under our desks, other than some horrible threat by "the Russians." This confused me because my grandparents had come from Russia – actually Ukraine – 50 years before and they didn't seem to be a threat to anyone.

Walt Disney created my generation's hope for a peaceful atomic future with his combination live action/animated film, *Our Friend, the Atom*. It included a graphic demonstration of a nuclear reaction, using hundreds of mousetraps, each set with two ping pong balls. To show how the power of the nuclear explosion builds, the host threw one ping pong ball – representing a neutron – into the array. This set off the mousetrap it hit, unleashing two balls, which then unleashed four, then an ever-increasing chaotic storm of bouncing balls.

Instead of putting me at peace, for months I lived in terror that some stray neutron would accidentally bump into another and – just like those ping pong balls – trigger an unstoppable nuclear explosion. In my mind, it could happen anywhere, any time. Disney may have meant the program as reassurance, but it filled me with an ongoing existential dread.

When Life magazine ran a story on atmospheric bomb tests. I glimpsed the vivid color photos over my much-older sister's shoulder as she read and said, "Oh, look at those pretty sunsets!" She whipped around on me, snapping, "They aren't pretty and they aren't sunsets!" I later snuck that issue to study. Nothing in the article spoke to the destructive power represented by the photographs.

And yes, they still looked pretty to me.

About that time, someone wrote to advice columnist Ann Landers and asked her thoughts on life after a nuclear war. I remember reading that she did not want to survive it and hoped she would be in the first group of people killed. That shocked me. If The Bomb hit, Ann Landers preferred to be killed by it rather than living? What kind of advice was that?

Science fiction movies fed my generation frightening images of radiation mutations such as Godzilla.[1] Books of post-apocalyptic science fiction stories kept me up late reading and awake long after I finished as they painted indelible images of the worst that could happen in the wake of a nuclear war: societal break down, earth's surface uninhabitable, survivors living in underground squats in the New York subway tunnels, mutant babies, cannibalism, and worse. Humanity would morph into things we didn't want to imagine, though obviously a lot of writers did.

That's the future I believed would await me if someone in Russia pushed The Button. I was young and wanted to survive, but Ann Landers' perspective haunted the edges of my thoughts as perhaps having some merit.

In 1959, the Chicago White Sox baseball team won their first pennant since 1919. My family sat in front of TV in the room next to my bedroom, noisily celebrating with the rest of the city. I'd already gone to bed for the night.

Suddenly, air raid sirens went off and did not stop. I knew what that meant. Terrified, I huddled in my bed, waiting for my parents to lead me down into the basement to give us a chance at surviving the atomic blast that was clearly on its way. We had only minutes until The Bomb landed and life as we knew it ended; why were they still watching TV?

When no one came to get me, I worked up the nerve and broke into their jubilation to announce, "The Russians are about to drop The Bomb on us and we have to get down into the basement now!"

They erupted in gales of laughter, saying the sirens were sounding because the Sox won the pennant. I pointed out there had been 20 minutes between them winning and the sirens going off, so obviously the two things had nothing to do with each other and the Russians were taking advantage of this opportunity to attack us while we weren't paying attention.

That provoked another wave of laughter.

I was ordered back to my room, where I lay awake for the next several hours, unable to trust my family's reassurances, ready to sprint to the basement at the first sign of atomic catastrophe. In the ensuing days and weeks, my actions that night became a favorite family anecdote. My siblings ribbed me mercilessly. But I didn't think I'd been wrong to maintain my nuclear vigilance, instead insisting that Mayor Daley had been a jerk to celebrate a baseball win with such a mixed metaphor.

In eighth grade, my Holocaust-surviving science teacher took sadistic glee in describing the impact of roentgens, a measure of radiation, on the human body. He'd elongate the word with a growl at the beginning and a hiss at the end – "grrrroentgennnsssss" – then smile a wicked smile and wiggle his tongue under his false teeth to scare us even more. His lectures on what Russian-released radiation would do to our chromosomes and vivid descriptions of just a few of the possible mutations made one girl run crying out of class to the bathroom, where she threw up.

Provoked in part by my science teacher's sadistic radiation musings, I entered the school's annual science fair with a model bomb shelter. I constructed a cutaway structure out of my brother's Block City blocks (an early Lego-like toy), added dollhouse furniture, peopled it with clothespin dolls, and added "supplies" by drawing brand names on tiny cardboard squares. For text, I pasted up another of Life's Atomic Age features, this one on how to build a bomb shelter. My exhibit had zero scientific merit and the judges mercifully avoided comment, but at least it provided me with means of expressing my nuclear angst.

By high school, other interests superseded the atom bomb for my attention. I sang in Symphonic Choir, twice wrote the book for our annual original school musical, pulled good enough grades, and even did a bit of dating. Mandatory science classes consisted of biology and chemistry, so I received no more training in the terrors of grrrroentgennnssss.

At the University of Illinois, I majored in journalism and broadcast communications, minored in speech/theatre, worked at student radio and TV stations. As a member of the first group of females admitted to Sigma Delta Chi,[2] the journalism society (previously fraternity), I became the first female co-editor of the *Illini Tumor* – "An Outgrowth of the Student Body" – a Homecoming weekend satire paper that raised our funding for the year. Then I became a copywriter for two local radio outlets while still an undergrad. I talked my way into assisting WGN-TV during their remote broadcast of the state high school basketball tournament – an annual event at the U of I – and as payment, I was given a summer job as an in-house temp secretary at WGN's Chicago studios. There, I parlayed my proximity to real TV producers into the sale of skits to *Bozo's Circus* – my first professional writing credits.

One month after leaving college, I landed a job in the promotions department at WGBH in Boston, where I wrote press releases for, among others, Julia Child. Frustrated at not being able to advance my career as quickly as I thought I deserved, one year later I joined a Cambridge-based drug education publishing house that dealt marijuana out of its loading dock. It quickly landed a contract to record the first-ever in-classroom training videos on drug-related issues for use by the US Army – and I was the only person on staff with any TV production experience.

So at 23, I became one of two producers assigned to create an eight-program drug education video series for the military. I lived out of Ft. Sam Houston in Texas and worked at Brooke Army Medical Center TV, where I wrote scripts, rehearsed actors, and interviewed experts. We took road trips down the west coast and through four countries in Europe, shooting footage at Army bases and in treatment facilities.

My salary bumped up, I received a generous per diem, exotic travel, creative freedom within the subject matter, and a major credit for my resume. Everyone agreed that I was on a fast track to an astounding future.

But I was miserable. Traveling so much from Boston to Texas to wherever, rarely at home, I fell out of contact with friends, developed no new relationships, and experienced no inner peace. On the road, I turned to casual sex and serious food in an attempt to feel connected. Neither worked. The sex proved forgettable but the food stuck around as I gained an astonishing amount of weight.

While in Boston preparing for a production trip to the Far East, I took a step I'd long been terrified of: I "came out" with another woman. I considered it a breakthrough to my inner truth. She – a colleague at work – immediately and hysterically declared herself straight, even as I knew I'd changed my self-definition.

A few days later, I lost my job. Our encounter did not factor into the decision. She swore she'd said nothing to anyone, and true, there were financial problems on the Army project, where my position was junior to the other producer, who was also the company's vice president. Whatever the reason, I suddenly found myself unemployed.

I rejoiced. Perfect timing.

It was spring, 1973 – the early days of the burgeoning Gay Liberation Movement. An actor friend had just been cast in a political play about gay people. The New York production was having major impact in New York and the Boston company still needed one woman. He brought me to rehearsal and I didn't even audition; the director just handed me the script and I started saying lines and writing down the blocking. Thus, only a week after I came out, I became a gay activist, part of the company of the Boston stage production of Jonathan Katz's *Coming Out! – A Documentary History of Gay Women and Men in the United States*.

The show proved an astounding success, performing to sold-out, standing room only crowds of people who drove as far as 200 miles to see it. The ovations we received often lasted five minutes or longer. Propelled by the explosive impact of this groundbreaking play, I suddenly found myself a celebrity within the gay community. Among other activities, I:

- hosted public fundraising events for gay groups.
- helped found the *Gay Community News (GCN)*, a weekly print newspaper.
- wrote the Media Message column for *GCN*, which allowed me to coach an entire movement on strategies, tactics, and attitudes for dealing with the media, as well sharing successes or places where protest letters and phone calls were needed.
- founded Gay Media Action as a media-response group.
- led surprise confrontations known as "zaps," protests, negotiations, and consciousness raising sessions with every media organization in the greater Boston area.
- produced and hosted *Closet Space*, a weekly broadcast radio program on WCAS-FM, Cambridge. As I cheerfully announced at the top of each show, *Closet Space* was "For and about the gay community… but if you're straight, it's okay to listen. After all, *we're* not prejudiced!"
- traveled to distant gay conferences and shared my media perspective, empowering groups to know how to successfully communicate with local broadcast and print news outlets about homophobia and fairness.
- booked a wide range of gay activists on local TV and radio stations.[3] Only after scheduling appearances for most of the local Boston movement leaders did I begin to take occasional opportunities for myself.

My work brought me to the attention of the National Gay Task Force (NGTF)[4] in New York. At the invitation of their Media Director, Ron Gold, I started commuting to New York City for meetings with executives at the three major networks, where we lobbied for fair, honest representation of gay women and men on television – at the time, something that was completely nonexistent.

In August, 1974, NGTF learned of a planned episode of *Marcus Welby, M.D.*, a doctor drama starring Robert Young and James Brolin that was then the top-rated show on TV. With the unconscious homophobia so common at the time, it presented a high school teacher who took his young charges on a camping trip and molested one of the boys. It featured such lines from the boy's father as, "Those people belong *in* jail. *Under* the jail. Now I understand murder!"

Ron Gold called to tell me of the show and that he had his hands full dealing with the network and coordinating with our west coast representative. Could I handle communicating with the activists?

You bet! Ron gave out my phone number and I charged into action. Gay activists from around the country called, desperate to know what they could do. We'd engage in lengthy strategizing sessions and I'd give them their marching orders for dealing with their local station. I wrote out the media negotiating strategies I'd developed, creating a 5-page handout that I mailed to activists around the country. I used the *Gay Community News* and *Closet Space* to keep the New England community informed of what was happening. I met repeatedly with the local ABC station general manager to convince him to drop the episode, which would represent an enormous loss of revenue to the network.

Every step of the way, I was kept fully informed of what was happening at ABC's New York headquarters by a leather queen doing advertising database entry in the company's basement. He accessed a free tie-line phone and called me long distance, every day, on the company's dime, to tell me the latest ad buys and drops. I'd then call the executive in charge of *Welby* advertising and drop into the conversation my latest knowledge. It made him nuts that I knew these things – sometimes before he did. ABC turned their executive offices and staff inside out trying to catch the leaker, but they never thought to check their minion in the basement.

The episode eventually aired in highly revised but still offensive form. Network promos filled more than half the advertising slots, meaning half the time on this top-rated program went unsold. The other half of the ad time was bought by lowball sponsors like Poligrip denture adhesive. Seven ABC stations refused to air the episode, including Boston and Philadelphia – a huge financial blow to the network. Activists as far away as Moscow, Idaho, used the opportunity to open up discussion on gay representation with their local media outlets. My strategies proved brutally effective, making history as we staged the first media protest by a minority group that commanded the attention of the entire entertainment industry.[5]

About this time, I started looking for a paying media job in Boston. I felt good about my recent media accomplishments – *Closet Space*, the *Welby* protest, public service announcements I wrote and recorded for the local NBC affiliate, and several installments of the half-hour public service TV program *Catch 44* on WGBH's sister-station, WGBX, Channel 44. But I neglected to account for the nature of my activist work and the sad fact that no mainstream media outlet in Greater Boston would dare risk giving me a job. I'd made myself unemployable in my chosen field.

So when, four months later, Ron Gold left NGTF pleading exhaustion, I accepted the group's invitation to move to New York and take his place as media director. In fast order, I made presentations in front of major industry groups and conferences, did interviews with WNYC-TV and radio stations, wrote media policy for groups around the country, attended board meetings and fundraisers, tried to keep my balance amidst the internecine grudge matches between New York gay and lesbian political groups... and burned out. Ten months after starting this exciting new job, I gave notice, saying I wanted to become a freelance writer. Movement honchos smirked and wondered aloud what the *real* story was.

But I'd always wanted to be a writer and my upward serendipity continued. My last week at NGTF, I got a call from the editor of *Michael's Thing*, a well-produced if more than slightly scandalous gay men's bar guide that featured tasteful full frontal shots of hot male nudes in every issue. When the editor asked, "Do you know any freelance writers?" I responded, "Next week I'll be one." While he seemed dubious about any "political" lesbian being willing to even acknowledge such a disreputable men's rag, let alone write for it, he told me to come in for an interview the following Monday.

Though it might have been considered controversial among hard-core activists, *Michael's Thing* represented a big break for me: the chance to write regularly for a New York publication. It might not be *The New Yorker*, but it was nicely printed on slick paper and would allow me to build my portfolio of clips.

Practicality beat out politics. I became the first lesbian and only second woman to write for the magazine, the other being a self-described fag hag who penned the astrology column.

I quickly began providing up to half a dozen articles per issue, then negotiated my way into a bylined column, *Unexpurgated Lotman.*[6] In it, I provided a running narrative of lesbian life in the Big Apple, writing the equivalent of a gay *Sex and the City* before Sarah Jessica Parker hit puberty.

Now sporting minor celebrity writer status, I was approached by the *Village Voice* – then the epitome of hip counterculture reporting. Would I be interested in writing some lesbian-themed articles for them? You betcha! I published several articles with the *Voice*, most notably, "I Was the Dyke at My High School Reunion," about going to my 10th high school reunion and putting on a big red GAY button. This was in 1975, a mere six years after the Stonewall Rebellion kicked off the gay liberation movement, and long before lesbians rented matching tuxedos to go to their prom.

Suddenly, I was "a thing" in New York City. Journalist Pete Hamill cited my article in his *New York Post* column as proof of Rupert Murdoch's intent to turn the *Voice* – his latest publishing acquisition – into a scandal sheet. (Pete had obviously read the title, but not my article.) I got invited to chichi loft parties with publishers and producers. Editors took me out to lunch in good restaurants and asked me for my book proposal. The *Voice* printed letters to the editor on my article three weeks in a row, and forwarded fan mail that included a thank you note from feminist Kate Millet and an unambiguous pass from a leggy, China-blue-eyed model, which I definitely caught. When she and I went out, her looks stopped every room into which we walked. I was the envy and/or fantasy object of every straight man who saw us together.

As a result of my growing national visibility, I got flown to UCLA to speak at a gay conference. While in Los Angeles, I was introduced to an agent who wanted to represent me as a writer for film and TV. I accepted, and six weeks later moved to LA. Because of my activist contacts, doors opened for me all over town. Norman Lear's production company (*All in the Family, Maude*) asked for my input to a new gender-reversal series, *All That Glitters.* The Los Angeles Actor's Theatre grabbed me for their in-house playwriting workshop and produced my first play, *Pearls that Coalesce,* within five months of my hitting town. I received ten stage productions in my first 18 months in LA and in the theatre world, developed a reputation as a hot writer.

On the personal front, I maintained ongoing relationships with both a woman and a man. (No, we didn't, so stop right there. They knew each other and knew about each other, but were kept completely separate.) Even though Hollywood refused to crack open to me, life seemed rich and filled with promise.

Then I fell into an obsessive non-relationship with someone who was happily settled with someone else. (This is the kind of situation that women look back upon and wonder at how stupid we must have been.) I overthrew my two existing relationships to clear the decks for this one, which never really happened. But that didn't stop me from acting really, really badly. I stalked before we used the term, inserted myself into the couple's life, spread emotional poison in my wake, and generally went out of control in ways I still don't understand.

When finally called on my bad behavior and told over a farewell exchange-of-artifacts lunch to never again darken the happy couple's door, through a stiff upper lip I said, "I'll be okay. I'm about to go out of town to get some writing done."

As though that explained anything.

I drove home, sobbing, but pulled myself together just enough to keep a planned first meeting with Jay Levin, editor of a new publication called *LA Weekly*. He read my clips and expressed interest in having me write for him. Needing to buy time, I said, "I'm going out of town for about a week to get some writing done, but when I return I'll check in and see if you have an assignment."

Then, having told the same lie twice, I figured I really did need to get out of town and maybe even do some writing. I called an old friend from Boston I hadn't seen for several years and got an automated message with a forwarding number that had an area code I didn't recognize. When I called this new number and she answered, I defaulted to an old game and opened our conversation, "Yes or no?" She said, "Yes! Absolutely!"

And that's how I found myself, that night, on a red eye flight to Harrisburg, Pennsylvania. It was Friday, March 23, 1979.

CHAPTER 2

GROUND ZERO AT ARMAGEDDON

Jeanne[7] greeted me at the Harrisburg Airport Saturday morning with a big smile and a hug. She and I had known each other since we worked together on an English as a Second Language coloring book for that Boston publishing house. She'd moved from Boston only three months before with her husband of six months, an airplane mechanic who'd landed a job at the Harrisburg airport. She'd always been the one in our group of friends who provided the maximum comfort after any relationship distress. As soon as I saw her, without preamble, I broke down and sobbed out my tale of woe.

Jeanne laughed reassuringly and said, "You've come to the right place to cool out. Middletown is really 'middle town.' Nothing important ever happens here."

We drove to the suburban townhouse she and her husband rented and I settled into their spare bedroom. Next day, I leased a typewriter to continue work on a musical political satire I'd been writing – the reason I'd given others for this sudden trip. Jeanne and Jim went off to their jobs and I had the days to write, the evenings to share cooking and conversation, the nights to cry myself to sleep. My friends lived media-less lives, using their one radio to occasionally listen to classical music, nothing more. It felt like I was on a retreat or, more likely, a therapeutic self-internment.

Five days after I arrived, late afternoon, I dashed across the street into a neighborhood mini-mart to secure a suitable number of calories to suppress my still-raging emotions. A nicely-dressed young man paid for his newspaper as he listened to the middle-aged cashier rattle on in a flat Midwestern accent.

"Well, my husband works there," she stated authoritatively, "and he said they told him it was about the same amount of radiation as you would get with an X-ray. Just a few milly-somethings."

"Millirems?" the man asked.

"Yeah, that's it," she said.

I butted in, "Radiation? Did something happen?"

The man nervously jerked his thumb over his shoulder. "Accident over at the N-plant this morning. Radiation leak."

The cashier jumped right in. "Oh, but my husband works there and it's OK, they've got it under control and there is nothing to worry about, that's what they told him."

Using my best big city cynicism, I replied, "And you believed them?"

I could have bit my tongue because I saw her face drain white and her eyes widen; she really did need to believe them.

I turned to the man. "Where did it happen?"

"Three Mile Island."

"Where's that?"

He stared at me. "Don't you know?"

"No, I'm just visiting here."

He pointed over my shoulder. "Over there. About a mile. You can see the cooling stacks from the playground."

I forgot all about my snack and stepped outside. There were the cooling towers, looming over the swing sets, the houses, the trees, just down the road. How had I not noticed them before?

Then the freelance writer in me wondered whether the story had gone national, and if so, how I might use this accidental proximity to my advantage.

When Jeanne got home from work, I couldn't wait to ask, "Did you hear about the accident?" She had, of course, but we could not comprehend its magnitude or importance, and without a TV set in the house, the growing hysteria remained outside our consciousness. The scene repeated itself when Jim arrived. He'd talked about it with the guys at work, but they all seemed to think it was no big deal and the media was waaaay out of control. By the time dinner ended, we'd exhausted our thin supply of information and paid the accident no further attention.

Calls started coming in the next morning, friends and relatives from around the country urging Jeanne and Jim to get out. Jeanne ran interference, laughingly reassuring the callers that there was no real danger, it was all media exaggeration, thanks for their concern but everyone was fine. Then they left for work as usual.

With *LA Weekly* in mind, I decided it was time to exercise my freelance chops. I put the musical on hold and walked about a mile into Middletown. I really enjoyed the Pennsylvania springtime air, breathing deeply of snowmelt and the quickening earth.

Middletown was tiny – I think it had one stop light that only blinked, surrounded by a small cluster of weather-beaten buildings. I spotted a diner and went in. As I slid onto a stool at the counter, I realized that by looking over the shoulder of the man seated next to me, I would be staring into a TV news mini-cam. The man, a reporter, talked into his mic with solemn self-importance, held silent for a beat, then abruptly got up and left, cameraman close behind.

The waitress waited for them to exit before she rushed to me. "Isn't it exciting?" she gushed. "They're from Philly This morning we had newspaper guys from Baltimore. They've been asking all of us what we think about the accident."

I asked her what kind of responses she and the others gave. She shrugged. "People don't have much to say. OK, it happened. What else is there?"

What else, indeed? I tried to find out. I bought a newspaper and read it while waiting outside for a bus. The *Harrisburg Evening News* carried more than five full pages on the accident. More media overreaction, I thought, smug in my cynicism.

When I got on the bus, the driver shouted, "That's right, get out of the radiation, fast!" Then he laughed. Two people in the front seats laughed with him. I soon discovered that every time a new passenger got on board, he welcomed them the exact same way, and everyone laughed heartily all over again.

As I took my seat, a middle aged woman next to me chimed in, "Did you hear that all pregnant women within five miles have been asked to get out?"

An adolescent girl piped up, "You'd think they'd have fabric or something to protect people. I mean, if you could see the rays coming at you, like black stuff, maybe you could protect yourself. But how can you protect yourself against something you can't even see?"

They went on like that, treating the purported disaster as excuse for some kind of social bee, a shared topic of conversation between strangers who otherwise would never speak to one another. They didn't seem to think that anything was involved other than a little problem down at the electric plant, something that got blown out of proportion by big city reporters.

In Harrisburg, Jeanne and I commiserated over a carafe of wine. She told me that many of her co-workers had fled to family hundreds of miles away. Still, we did not worry as we discussed most people's easy acquiescence to the official reassurances.

"They believe nothing is wrong, that it will all go away, it's being handled," she said. "They're saying, 'Everything must be all right, because if it wasn't someone would tell us about it.'" As two olde Boston hippies, we agreed that it made no sense to trust government officials, yet recognized no contradiction between this skepticism and our own willingness to be soothed by the official line. Instead, we polished off the carafe.

Boarding the bus back to Middletown, I tried not to think of the fact that we were going closer, closer to Three Mile Island. After all, the worst was over. At least, that's what they were telling us.

When Jim came home, his tension snapped us into something more real. "They still haven't got it cleaned up," he said. "Some of my co-workers have family members working there. They tell me it's not good."

I thought about booking a return flight, but let it go. I still needed small town peace and quiet before facing the emotional mess waiting for me back in LA.

The next morning, I awoke to another beautiful Pennsylvania springtime day. Despite the brisk temperature, I opened up the window in front of my typewriter and, taking deep breaths of fresh air, started to work on the musical. But less than one page into the rewrite, I heard a garbled loudspeaker from the front of the house. Unable to understand what was being said, I ran downstairs and flung open the door to hear:

"CLOSE ALL YOUR DOORS AND WINDOWS AND STAY AWAY FROM THEM. STAY INSIDE AND DO NOT LEAVE YOUR HOMES UNLESS IT IS ABSOLUTELY NECESSARY."

I slammed the door, ran upstairs and shut the window, almost afraid to touch it for fear of contamination. The phone rang. It was Jim. "We're getting out."

More radioactivity had leaked. The airport was closed. The governor "suggested" evacuation within a five-mile radius of the plant. That meant us. Jim asked me to call Jeanne in Harrisburg to tell her he was coming to pick her up, then they'd come for me. It took me a dozen tries to get a line through to her. She was set to go, her office already a ghost town.

As I hung up, I desperately needed to hear a voice from someone in my life who was safe. I'd left town so quickly, with so much shame, I hadn't let anyone know where I was going. I suspected they'd laugh at my current tale of woe and accuse me of trying to perpetrate some overly dramatic hoax.

I should only be so lucky.

Thoroughly panicked, I dialed for long distance but couldn't get a line, only a high-pitched wailing noise, like a siren, cycling over and over again. I never knew that telephones could make noises like that. I slammed the receiver down and tried again, and again, never getting through, my panic growing as I began to realize exactly how bad a mess I'd gotten myself into.

Alone in the house with a malfunctioning nuclear reactor only one mile away, dead phones, no car, public transportation suspended, no way of knowing if that thing might blow up or how much radiation I'd already been subjected to, everything I had been made afraid of in the 1950's as coming from the Russians suddenly threatened me from only one mile away, courtesy my own government and the local utility. Civilization's fall crystallized into a single thought: "If that thing explodes, this house has no basement in which to hide from the blast."

I wandered from room to room, waiting for my friends to show up and get me out, my mind obsessively replaying everything I knew about nuclear. I remembered that eighth grade science teacher going on about roentgens and radiation damage from nuclear bombs in the aftermath of a blast. It wasn't just the thermonuclear devastation that could kill us; the worst came later, when radiation ate our lives from the inside out. "Radiation can't be seen, smelled, tasted, felt, perceived with normal human senses," he told us, relishing the fear in our eyes as he elaborated on the deadly consequences of invisible exposure: "It gets into your food, your water, your chromosomes, it mutates your genes, your babies will be deformed if they get born at all, you'll all get cancer and die young and the human race will soon be over."

Based on what he'd taught us so well those many years ago, if the radiation release from Three Mile Island was bad enough, I didn't need to fear a blast; I was already as good as dead.

Then I caught sight of myself in the bathroom mirror and stared at my face, directly into my eyes, and wondered: As I watch, will I see my hair fall out? Blisters boil through my flesh? Skin melt off my cheekbones? When the reactor explodes, will there be a split-second when time freezes just before I evaporate to atoms? If so, will I understand in that final flash that the unthinkable has happened and that life on Earth has changed, inexorably, forever? Only I won't be around to see it?

When will it happen? Now? Now??? Maybe NOW...?

Unable to look away, I began playing a game from early childhood. While driving in the car with my mother, every time we stopped at a red light, I'd try to guess when it would turn green by counting down: "Three... two... one..." and then I'd point, trying to pinpoint the exact moment it changed and, in the rare instances when it worked, pretending I'd done some magic to make it happen.

Here at Three Mile Island, staring at myself in a bathroom mirror, I became transfixed trying to pinpoint the exact moment the nuclear reactor would explode and take me with it. I counted out loud, "Three... two... one..." and then pointed at myself in the mirror, hoping to nail the moment when I would be no more. When I continued to live, I suppressed a bizarre kind of disappointment and told myself, "No, not this time. Maybe next?" Then I resumed counting: "Three... two..."

The phone rang, jolting me back from the brink of madness. Jim, calling from a payphone. He'd picked up Jeanne and they were on their way to get me. He asked me to pack only the barest essentials and be ready to leave in an hour.

22

I paced obsessive figure eights through the house, a slow, intense, non-stop loop between the rooms, jaw clamped shut for fear I'd start screaming and never be able to stop. But that internal monologue played relentlessly in my head: Was I about to die? Was I dead already? Would there be any warning if it was going to blow? When would it be? Now? NOW??? Three… two…"

As I wandered, picking up a few things and throwing them into a pillowcase – more compact than my suitcase – I was terrified to go into the bathroom for my toiletries and risk falling into that mirror again. I passed the doorway probably a dozen times before I covered my eyes with one hand, rushed in, grabbed my things, and ran out. Then I stared at my toothbrush for several minutes, unable to figure out how to pack it. See, it was wet. How does one pack a wet toothbrush in a pillowcase when there's a leaking nuclear reactor just down the road?

So much for my IQ.

Jim and Jeanne arrived. We rushed around, packing the car, never looking directly at each other, not talking about more than the most mundane aspects of evacuation. There was a smog-like haze in the air, thick and humid. Caused by radiation? Carrying fall-out? How many roentgens in a millirem? Overhead, a bird chirped. At least it wasn't dead. Yet.

We fit three adults, a cat, and the typewriter into a VW Beetle, then evacuated 150 miles to a friend of Jim's who served as caretaker at a Christian retreat. We arrived unannounced but not unexpected. No one spoke of where we'd come from. Or why.

That night, in the cozy Civil War era home, I set up an area for writing and was about to restart the musical when

Jeanne stuck her head into my room. "There's going to be a news special on TV in a few minutes." A moth to the media flame, I needed to finally learn the basis for the warnings we'd ignored for 2-1/2 days.

There's something unnerving about learning that what happened to you that morning is the international lead news story of the day. But there was news anchor Walter Cronkite – "the most trusted man in America" – addressing a problem from my immediate life on national television.[8] He showed the Middletown street I'd walked down... was it only yesterday? An ambulance making the same loudspeaker announcement I'd heard that very morning. Then the facts we'd not yet learned: xenon gas, hydrogen bubble in the reactor, possible explosion and yes, radiation releases.

The picture shifted and there were all the little nuclear officials at a press conference, running around like clowns in a three-ring circus, contradicting each other, telling us to feel secure when the terror in their eyes showed that they were scared, too.

A Nuclear Regulatory Commission (NRC) press aide named Joseph Fouchard faced the accumulated media of the world to read an announcement. Sweat pouring down his pasty face, hands shaking, voice trembling, he told us not to worry, that everything was under control.

Not a very convincing performance.

A nuclear consultant/apologist named Dr. Lapp assured us that this was not a disaster or catastrophe because "no one was injured." A Dr. Pollard from the Union of Concerned Scientists rebutted him, quoting a member of the Nuclear Regulatory Commission as once having said, "If it involves me, it's a catastrophe; if it's anyone else, we'll discuss it."

LIBBE HaLEVY

President Carter had been briefed but was off on a political trip to Milwaukee.

Two doctors discussed the effects of excess radiation on human tissue.

Then Cronkite wrapped it up, looking angrier than I'd seen him since the 1968 Democratic National Convention.

We turned off the TV and sat around it, very quiet. Jeanne and Jim held onto each other lightly, but with meaning. The others were respectful and gave us our space. I sat alone, a stranger in this land, accidentally in the middle of an accident.

That night, I slept fitfully. When I awoke next morning, one of those inexplicable miracles of the creative process had taken place: a song appeared intact in my mind, music as well as lyrics. I wrote it down and recognized it as a father's song to his daughter, entitled "I'm Scared, Too." I thought it the best thing I'd ever written.

But it did not fit with the political satire.

Then I realized that I was living a political satire; I didn't need to write one. Indeed, political satire is a thing of the moment. In theatre, that kind of work dates quickly. I wanted to create a musical that had a chance of a long life – something I feared I no longer had ahead of me.

We'd been told that the devices to measure release of radiation didn't work, so no one knew how badly we'd been exposed. I presumed it was because this monitor – something I imagined as kind of a thermostat – had been supplied by the lowest bidder. As a result (so I thought), at the critical time it malfunctioned, meaning we would never know any specifics about the radiation released at Three Mile Island.[9]

I called Jay Levin at *LA Weekly*, told him where I was and asked if he was interested in a first-hand story. After a

25

long pause, he assured me he was very interested in an article and asked how I was. I heard the first half of that sentence but ignored the rest and started telling him what was going on. All that night and into the next day, I pounded out an article about what I'd been living through, then drove it to the nearest FedEx office, overnight delivery being an amazing new development in the business world.

To put whatever life I had left to the best possible use, I dumped the musical I'd been working on – ironically entitled *Armageddon* – and started on the new show. I wrote obsessively, using "I'm Scared, Too" as a starting point to create a musical focused on the universal truth of human emotions. I imagined an amusement park where all the rides were emotional confrontations and a manipulating ringmaster who offered you your heart's desire as a trick to entrap you into an inescapable hell. I named the show after the amusement park: *KAZOO*.

Only much later did I learn that at the turn of the 20th Century, Three Mile Island had been an amusement park.

Convinced that I might soon be dead, I wrote as if my sanity depended upon it... which it did. During that time, I gained five pounds from stress-related eating and struggled with nightmares that demolished my ability to sleep. But at least I no longer obsessed on my relationship woes! That problem receded to irrelevance, except as the reason I'd started on this impossible sequence of events in the first place.

Eight days later, Harrisburg airport reopened and I left the evacuation site to prep myself for the next day's flight out. On the way, I stopped in Middletown and saw newly printed T-shirts being sold out of the trunk of someone's car. "I Survived Three Mile Island," they read, over a badly drawn graphic of the cooling towers. By then, with my weight gain, I needed a medium if not a large, but all they had were smalls. I bought two.

Standing around for the T-shirts, I fell into the animated conversation surrounding me. Everyone was abuzz over Johnny Carson on *The Tonight Show* and the jokes he'd been telling about Three Mile Island. People repeated the punch lines of his Carnac the Magnificent routine, which consisted of a turban'ed swami (Carson) putting an envelope up to his forehead, giving an answer, then opening it up to read the question, which was the punch line:

A: Mop and Glow.

Q: Which floor wax was used by the Three Mile Island cleanup team?

A: Thanksgiving dinner at Three Mile Island.

Q: What do you call a two-pound turkey and a fifty-pound cranberry?

We laughed each time a joke was repeated, not because it was still funny, but because we recognized ourselves and our situation in what he was saying and shared our inexpressible pain through laughter. We LOVED Johnny Carson, because he wasn't stuck with us at Three Mile Island, but he reached into the middle of our nightmare and stood up for us on national television. His humor cheered us up and we cheered him on. Those laughs helped us keep it together.

I learned about a press conference with the Nuclear Regulatory Commission being held right then in the Middletown High School, so I crashed it, citing *LA Weekly* as my publication. On a stage at one end of a high school gym, the "experts" and their PR flacks fielded questions from about 100 international reporters.

The weirdest sight in the gym was far upstage, where what looked like stenographers were typing on small machines with large cone-shaped devices directly in front of them. Were they speaking into a recorder? Breathing enriched or purified air? If so, why didn't any of the nuke industry or government reps use these devices? I never did learn their purpose.

While the moderator fielded questions from reporters around me, I didn't even raise my hand, feeling more like a victim than a reporter. I overheard the muttered conversations of many of these news professionals. They quietly admitted to each other that they were freaked out by their proximity to a story that had absolutely no respect for their press badges and could genuinely hurt them.

In the scrum of reporters and news sources, I honed in on a freelance photographer. After the press conference broke up, I hired him to take some "souvenir photos" of me at the local nuclear hotspot. I figured that this whole thing was so weird and improbable, if I couldn't prove where I'd been, no one would ever believe me.

We drove around to grab a number of shots. One photo shows me wearing one of those "I Survived Three Mile Island" T-shirts while standing on the edge of the Susquehanna River across from the reactor – which for all we knew was still leaking. The photographer hurried me through the set-up, saying, "I've been up here twice before and I'm already afraid that any offspring I have may end up looking like tadpoles."

Next day, early, I was on a plane heading back home. As we took off, a steep turn banked us directly over the nuclear reactors of Three Mile Island. I had no sense of relief at leaving, just a pending sense of doom at having to face the awfulness I'd left behind in LA as well as the unknown long term effects of what I had experienced in Middletown.

The flight back to Los Angeles stopped over in Chicago, where my mother lived. I called before I left Harrisburg and let her know I'd be passing through town. She met me at Midway airport for this sudden, unexpected reunion. I told her I'd just been in Pennsylvania, hoping she would catch my drift without the need for an explanation, but she responded, "Did you see our cousins in Pittsburgh?" When I told her exactly where I'd been, her face went ashen. She silently took my hand and held it, gently but with strength. It was probably the most intimate, loving contact of our adult lives.

When the plane left for LA, that sense of doom descended again and locked into place. The look in my mother's eyes brought home an absolute terror at what I was up against. Yes, I was on my way back to Los Angeles. I'd escaped Three Mile Island… but would I survive it?

CHAPTER 3

BACK TO NORMAL... NOT!

Back in Los Angeles, I went immediately to the *LA Weekly* office to work with Jay Levin on editing my article. While there, he handed me a copy of the previous week's paper. It featured an interview with a woman I'd never heard of, a pediatrician and anti-nuclear activist originally from Australia named Dr. Helen Caldicott. In the article, she stated that after exposure to low level radiation, leukemia could show up in five to seven years, hard tumors in 12 to 15 years.

A clock popped into the back of my brain and started counting down to what I feared was inevitable cancer.

From Dr. Caldicott's words, I began to understand the nuclear betrayal of my body. It might be years before any problem appeared, but I had no doubt that I was up against something very real... and terrifying.

I'd returned from Middletown with those "I Survived Three Mile Island" T-shirts. Desperate to let Johnny Carson know how important he'd been to us, I called the production office of *The Tonight Show* and demanded to talk to someone in power. Through ever-rising levels of influence, I told them where I'd been, that I had a present for Johnny from TMI, and that he needed to know the impact his humor had on us all so he would continue telling those jokes. I wouldn't take no for an answer.

Eventually, I was invited to the production offices, where I was welcomed by Johnny's executive producer, Freddie de Cordova. I repeated my story to him as he listened, gently accommodating someone he must have considered a bit of a motor-mouthing nutball. Then I gave him one of the T-shirts and asked him to give it to Johnny, which he said he would. I also gave him a list of jokes I'd written about Three Mile Island for Johnny's consideration. He explained that un-agented material could not be considered, but thanked me for thinking of them as he handed my pages back.[10]

That night, I eagerly watched the show, desperate for some acknowledgement, no matter how anonymous, that I had been there and said what I'd said. Nothing. Okay. That's showbiz. On to what was left of my tattered life.

When I saw friends, I tried to explain my situation, but they had no ability to comprehend what had happened to me or why it was such a big deal. Three Mile Island was on the other side of the country, so far away that it had quickly faded from their thoughts. As I pushed on, desperate to make myself and my panic understood, they tried to deflect their own nervousness by making light of it: "Isn't that just like you to be where the action is!" "Do you glow in the dark?" Then, in a more serious vein: "You're not contagious, are you?" as they slowly edged away.

Unable to deal with their well-meaning lack of under-standing, I stopped trying to talk about the experience. If anyone asked where I'd been, with a rape victim's sense of guilt I hid the truth and simply said, "Pennsylvania" or "back east." Even after the article appeared, *LA Weekly* was not yet in wide circulation, so most people in my life missed the story. I didn't bring it up.

"Post-traumatic stress" was not a widely known clinical term in 1979, but that's what I suffered from in the wake of Three Mile Island. I struggled with insomnia and nightmares, receded into isolation, terror, and compulsive behaviors. I couldn't concentrate on any writing project and for the first time in my life fumbled some deadlines.

I diverted myself through an ever-increasing number of bizarre behaviors: short-term, ill-conceived sexual encounters, sometimes with more than one partner in a single night. I'd sit in fast food restaurants staring at strangers as if daring them to ask me what was the matter so I could tell them, watch the horror grow on their face, and by this transference forestall my panic, if only for the length of that conversation. One day, I spent ten hours obsessing on the meaning of each letter of the alphabet. Most nights I drank too much and then drove home by the most dangerous roads I could find, entirely willing to "accidentally" drive off the cliffs of Mulholland, part of me convinced it would be a better solution than continuing the agony of not knowing what was going to happen to me as a result of Three Mile Island.

No one could tell me how much radiation had leaked or what the probable effect would be on my body. Courtesy my eighth grade science teacher's atomic horror stories, I knew that radiation devastated the reproductive system, mutating chromosomes and setting up the probability of birth defects. So on a daily basis I debated getting myself sterilized. I didn't want to run the risk of giving birth to a permanently disabled baby. I knew instinctively that I wasn't strong enough or "good" enough to deal with a special needs child (though that wasn't what we called them back then). Finally, after months of making myself crazy with this internal monologue, I resolved to simply be vigilant and not allow my body to give birth. Ever.

In this way, all my children died at Three Mile Island.

Time and distance did not help me regain my previous personality and lifestyle. Three Mile Island mule-kicked me out of the life I'd been living and into an alternate reality:

- Where I'd been outgoing and very public in my life before Three Mile Island, afterwards I hid, pretending that everything was fine when it absolutely wasn't.
- Where I'd confidently assumed positive outcomes to my endeavors, I now anticipated only failure, futility, doom.
- Where I'd been of robust health, high energy, and great stamina, I now found myself depleted, tired, unable to concentrate long enough to complete writing projects or market myself. I lived off my saving.
- Where before I'd embraced life, now I ran from it.
- I doubted everything I thought I knew, because Three Mile Island and my reaction to it proved that I didn't know anything about myself or the world in which I lived.

A therapist probably would have found me, at minimum, clinically depressed, but I wouldn't let a mental health professional close enough to diagnose me. I couldn't admit that things were as bad as they were. I feared that if I let it out to someone else, I'd lose control over my life, be forced to medication, or worse. But my life *was* spinning totally out of control and I didn't know how to stop it. I saw no way out of my despair.

Six months after Three Mile Island, still lost amid the fears and the flashbacks, my mother asked if I'd like to go to with her to Israel for the bar mitzvah of a family friend's grandson at the Western Wall. Ever since high school graduation, I'd sidestepped her traditional Jewish mother's appeal to visit The Promised Land. Now, with nothing on my horizon other than an endless black pit of near-suicidal depression, I figured, why not?

One week later, I flew out of Los Angeles to Israel, where I met up with my mother in Jerusalem. Other than a few bar mitzvah-related obligations, I was free to explore the country as I wished.

I wandered from Arab *suk* to religious sites to tourist traps to a kibbutz recommended by a sexual partner in LA. Everywhere, I spoke with people who had lived through far worse than a leaking nuclear reactor down the street. Holocaust survivors, Ethiopian refugees, war veterans, displaced Arabs – it seemed everyone told a tale of challenge, struggle, and survival. No one flinched as I spoke about Three Mile Island. They asked intelligent questions. They listened to my answers. Their honesty and openness stood in stark contrast to the wincing avoidance I faced back home when I tried to broach the subject.

I listened to them, too, and learned a complexity of life in Israel that does not translate through the media or the carefully curated bus tours. If there was a commonality among everyone I met, it was that they read, thought, talked, argued, connected on the issues of life large and small. I'd never been involved with such committed people. My time with them all – Jew, Arab, Christian, Muslim – felt more comfortable than anything I'd experienced since Three Mile Island.

My mother returned to the states but I remained in Jerusalem for another week. During that time, I fell in with a delegation of politicos from California that included Secretary of State Jesse Unruh, U.S. Representative Diane Watson, and California State Senate President Pro-Tem David Roberti. Besides sharing insights I'd gained about the country and guiding them to one of the more ethical jewelry stores in the Old City, I told them about my experience at Three Mile Island. I did not yet know the names of the nuclear reactors in California or even that we had any, but I could speak of the fear generated by TMI, the government mismanagement after the accident, the lack of accurate information, the absence of follow-up. Still in the depths of my own depression, I couldn't tell if what I said would make any impact upon their future energy policies, but the women really appreciated the unique jewelry they were able to buy in the 800-year-old store I showed them.

Israel left a deep impact on me. I treasured the honesty of the people and the welcome they provided. I flew back to the States determined to find a way to return to the country, possibly to live there.

In California, I worked hard at getting my life back on track and tried to get involved with anti-nuclear causes, with middling success. For most of those working in the movement, nuclear dangers were an abstract concept. I'd lived in fear of the effects daily, and my intense, readily accessed terror did not mesh with the headsets of those I met.

My volunteer time working with the anti-nuclear Alliance for Survival proved frustrating. In Los Angeles, proximity to the entertainment industry makes volunteer work for any "hot" non-profit fraught with ego and one-upmanship. For all the worthy goals listed by the organization, the people I dealt with seemed most interested in jockeying for position near celebrities at their upcoming Hollywood Bowl fundraising concert. I offered to tell my story – not for ego purposes, but to put the focus on the human element and the impact of the experience of Three Mile Island. No one wanted to hear it, not in the office and certainly not from any highly visible stage. Instead, like any other volunteer, I stuffed envelopes.

At the Bowl, I worked with the media, though I was forbidden to mention what had happened to me. I did meet Mike Gray, author of *The Warning: Accident at Three Mile Island*. He also co-author the script for *The China Syndrome*, which had premiered less than two weeks before TMI and told the story of corporate negligence leading to a nuclear accident – a film I could not yet bring myself to watch.[11] Mike was the only person with whom I confided my experience. We talked for about five minutes and exchanged contact information, though neither one of us ever followed up.

I kept trying to fit into this movement, with ever-declining results. The straw that broke it came at a big demonstration/rock concert/alternative marketplace, where images of the TMI cooling towers assailed me from bumper stickers, buttons, T-shirts, tote bags. Someone even crafted them as candles, allowing the purchaser to experience a literal – if benign – meltdown. I found the trivial overuse of this iconic image both irrelevant and overwhelming, as it retriggered my PTSD every time I saw another graphic depiction. People seemed to treat this commemoration of Three Mile Island as nothing more than an opportunity for a be-in, a fun social gathering out-of-doors on a Sunday afternoon.

I was way too heavy a vibe for this crowd. Without making a conscious decision, I moved away from anti-nuclear activism. Instead, I put energy into getting myself back to Israel.

My plans to leave the US coincided with the first anniversary of Three Mile Island. Wanting to sum up a year living under its nuclear shadow, I queried the *Los Angeles Times* about writing an Op-Ed piece. Under their general submission policy (send it in on spec, no guarantees of publication), I wrote a 700-word article in which I likened my experience at Three Mile Island to an episode of *The Twilight Zone*.

The *Times* not only accepted the article but promoted it in their radio ads. Publication of the piece exploded a firestorm of letters to the editor, and even a condescending op-ed countering my position, belittling my fears while reassuring readers that nuclear was "perfectly safe."

But all that meant little to me. By the time my op-ed hit, I was already on my way to Israel.

CHAPTER 4

LOOKING FOR PEACE IN ISRAEL

I settled onto Kibbutz Kfar Hanassi, located north of the Sea of Galilee, right across the River Jordan from the Golan Heights. Founded in 1949 as a border kibbutz, intentionally placed there as part of a line of national defense, it grew from a ragtag group of British, Polish, and Australian Zionists camping in the middle of a thistle-filled wilderness to a thriving community of about 800. After the Six-Day War in 1967, the kibbutzniks had a saying: "We used to be brave; then they moved the borders."

By the time I arrived, they'd long since abandoned their bomb shelters to storage, except for one converted into a British-style pub complete with lukewarm ale and a dartboard. For income, the kibbutz raised sheep and chickens, grew avocados and grapefruit for export to Europe, manufactured nuts, bolts, and screws. In exchange for six days of work each week, every kibbutz resident received housing, food, medical, support services (laundry, recreation, etc.), entertainment, and a small monthly stipend. They even got two weeks of paid vacation per year, with kibbutz-owned apartments around the country in which families could stay at no charge.

K'far Hanassi respected and supported its artists. Depending on their level of success and the financial contribution their art made to the kibbutz, members were given up to five days a week to concentrate on their painting, music, sculpture, or writing. One accomplished painter, Lawrence Marcuson, was on a year's sabbatical to travel, study abroad and gain new inspiration for his work, all supported by the kibbutz. His pictures graced the dining room walls and made me sorry I'd missed meeting him.

I'd signed up for an *ulpan*, a program designed to teach Hebrew to potential immigrants. Six days a week, half my time belonged to classroom study and half to work, which paid for my stay. My jobs consisted of the lowest rung of labor on the kibbutz hierarchy: cooking breakfast eggs for 800, ironing 200 shirts a day (plackets, cuffs, and collars only; everything else got sweated through in the relentless summer heat so we didn't bother with them), washing dishes, polishing floors, gardening. My favorite job, for which I awoke long before dawn, was pruning the grapefruit trees. We'd climb ladders to snip off dead wood, in the process plucking and eating magnificently ripe fruit that had eluded the harvest.

One of my first weeks on kibbutz, an article appeared in the *Jerusalem Post*, the country's largest English-language daily newspaper. It touted the marvels of Israel's move into nuclear energy and how important this was to the country's future. I glimpsed it over the shoulder of an obstreperous New Zealand *ulpanist* as he lingered over breakfast in the communal dining room.

My brain just about imploded. Over his loud protests, I snatched the newspaper from his hands, cut Hebrew class, and banged out a letter to the editor, which I promptly mailed. My belligerence and lack of tact that day almost got me ousted from the kibbutz until I confessed the source of my upset. Upon learning that I'd been at Three Mile Island, they let me off with a warning to shape up.

Eleven days later, while eating breakfast, one of the kibbutz old-timers walked up to me and said sternly, "Next time, don't say you're from Kfar Hanassi, you're only in the *ulpan*."

The *Jerusalem Post* had published my letter. As a result, I developed instant standing on the kibbutz. They acknowledged me as a writer, an activist, someone with an interesting past – not the usual teenaged *ulpanist*. I began receiving invitations to private family dinners. People wanted to sit next to me at communal meals and engage in conversation. Everywhere I went, people welcomed me as a refreshing addition to the community.

This brought me to the attention of a large extended family that included three founders of the kibbutz. One of them, Yisroel Avigdor, had been a teenaged member of the French Underground during World War II. Then in his late 50's, he worked actively within the Israeli Labor movement. His family "adopted" me for the length of my stay and Yisroel arranged several private, informal meetings with organizers within the Labor party so I could discuss my perspective on nuclear energy.

Quite a contrast to the reception I'd experienced in America.

I continued to prove difficult to the people around me, with a hair-trigger temper and an overwhelming desire to be left alone. About two months into my time on kibbutz, the entire *ulpan* took a day trip that included a harrowing descent down a sheer six-story cliff without benefit of equipment – safety or otherwise; a visit to a small Holocaust museum that featured heart-wrenching drawings of concentration camp scenes mad by an imprisoned Jewish political cartoonist, a man who later died in the gas chamber; and several snarly encounters with my teenaged Aussie classmates, who responded to the overwhelming pain of what they were witnessing with giggles, bad jokes, and physical roughhousing.

On the bus home, struggling on verge of tears from the intense emotions of the day, I suddenly flashed back to Three Mile Island. I saw myself standing in the bathroom, looking at myself in the mirror, waiting for the explosion, counting "Three... two... one..." In that moment, I burst out of the mental/emotional shell I'd been imprisoned in with a single thought: I am alive.

From what I now understand about Post Traumatic Stress Disorder (PTSD), under the emotional pressure created by that announcement coming down the street at Three Mile Island, I dissociated – psychologically separated from reality – because I couldn't handle what was happening. This was not a conscious choice but an instinctive, hard-wired survival mechanism. To compensate for the stress that followed, on some level I continued to come from this out-of-the-body place. Nothing around me mattered because I was just imagining it all! Merrily, merrily, merrily, merrily, the life I had been living was but a dream, and in truth, I was actually trapped back in Middletown, frozen in time, staring at myself in that bathroom mirror in the instant before I died. Since that horrifying moment, I'd spent 18 months subconsciously preventing anything from registering as real. It was as if I'd been living an imaginary flash-forward from the split-instant just before I died.

Under the pressure of that day in Israel, this protective delusion cracked. The long-held emotions flooded out, and I re-engaged with reality. I could feel my body tingle as muscles let go of their long-held emotional energy. I broke down crying and managed to sob out why, to which my Australian classmates responded, "Brilliant!" From that point on, in the isolated safety of the kibbutz environment, I began recovering a genuine sense of self. My PTSD wasn't over, but I'd discharged a major piece of it.

By late summer, with Yisroel's support, I'd published articles in international Labor Party publications, several letters to the editor of the *Jerusalem Post*, and was being approached as to my intentions regarding the country. Was I willing to make *aliyah*? Immigrate to Israel? Make that country my home? If so, Yisroel's associates offered me support, encouragement, connections. The government actively wanted Americans to come live in the country, and to that end provided all immigrants with housing, a stipend, language training, and job placement. As the country was a democracy, I would be able to speak freely on nuclear issues. All I had to do was stay.

It was tempting. As a product of the 60's, I grew up to believe that I was personally responsible for changing the world. Here I was being offered an opportunity to do just that. Israel is about the same size as New Jersey, with a population at the time of fewer than four million people. This represented enormous potential for an individual to make a difference. The country's culture encouraged conversation, debate, discussion, and since its founding accepted women as equal to men. While Hebrew would undoubtedly prove a challenge, especially for writing, the *Jerusalem Post* published daily in English and welcomed submissions from freelancers. Everything I wanted seemed within reach.

All four of my grandparents left their home countries in Eastern Europe to travel to America in search of a better life. Did I have the courage to give up America in search of a different kind of life? I'd left so much incompletion in the U.S. – relationships, writing projects, career intentions, my physical stuff. Was any of it important enough to return to? Or was it time to cut the cords and embrace a new country, one where I might be able to influence nuclear policy and, in so doing, genuinely change the world for the better?

All this remained up in the air as the *ulpan* ended and, with it, the time allotted to me at K'far Hanassi. It was September, when Jews celebrate the High Holy Days of Rosh Hashanah (the Jewish New Year) and Yom Kippur (Day of Atonement). Jews believe that during the week between these two days, God writes in the Book of Life all that will happen in the coming year. Though I was not religious, I traveled to Jerusalem to spend this time with the family friends whose son's bar mitzvah first brought me to the country.

A few days after Rosh Hashanah, I caught up with a movie that premiered after I left Los Angeles and that had finally made it to Jerusalem: Bob Fosse's *All That Jazz*. This paean to all things Broadway tells the story of a successful, charming, womanizing, pharmaceutical-addicted director/ choreographer as he rehearses a new Broadway musical, edits a film, and balances relationships with his ex-wife, mistress, and daughter. Lots of singing and dancing, too. Oh, and Jessica Lange appears as an elegantly attired Death.

In one scene near the end, the director – now pre-op for open heart surgery and trying to escape this reality – dances around in the hospital basement, splashing through puddles of water while wearing only an open-back gown. (It sort-of makes sense in context.) A high camera angle pivots down as he comes closer and looks up into the lens. As if beseeching God directly, he cries out to the heavens, "What's the matter – don't you like musical comedy?!"

Sitting alone in the darkened theatre half a world from Broadway, everything inside me rose up and screamed in my head, "He does! He does!"

When I returned to the family with whom I was staying, someone had just returned from the States and brought with him a pile of mail my mother did not consider important enough to forward to me. In it, I found an invitation to apply for the ASCAP musical theatre workshop, at the time the only developmental opportunity in the country for writers of new musicals. It was headed by legendary Broadway composer/lyricist Stephen Sondheim (*Sweeny Todd, Into the Woods*) and esteemed composer Charles Strouse (*Annie*).

I took it as a sign. Of course! I could stay in Israel and work towards a sane nuclear policy, or I could return to the States, launch my Three Mile Island musical to Broadway success, publicize the background behind it to raise consciousness of nuclear issues, *and then* move to Israel to work towards nuclear sanity!

It's perhaps a hallmark of my PTSD that I never considered this game plan seriously flawed. At the time, it seemed like I'd experienced a giant finger in the sky pointing me back towards America. I figured that with Divine Providence leading the way, I'd be back in Israel within 18 months, two years at most, with a lifetime income from royalties off a Broadway hit and a public profile that would guarantee that I'd have the ear of the media, if not the world. Maybe I'd even get to say something profound about nuclear issues on national television as I accepted my Tony™ Award for Best Musical of 1981!

Consumed with fulfilling what I by then thought of as My Destiny, I made up my mind: I'd go back to the States until I returned in musical theatre triumph to The Promised Land!

Oy!

CHAPTER 5

THE ANTIDOTE TO THREE MILE ISLAND IS... BROADWAY?

On the slender thread of my Broadway fixation, I hustled to get back to America in time for the ASCAP workshop. I ignored the fact that the deadline for submission to the program was long past, the start date imminent, and I had no guarantee of participation. Certain that I would not, could not be refused, I wrote a plea to be accepted to the program in the form of an elaborate musical theatre scene, and paid exorbitant rates to expedite its delivery to the heads of the program half a world away.[12] Then I packed up, leaving behind what I couldn't carry on my back, and zipped through Europe in record time on my way to Rendezvous with Musical Theatre Destiny!

Thus, when I got to New York, I was shocked, I tell you, shocked! to discover that ASCAP had been deeply unimpressed with my frantic attempts to crash its program. The secretary in charge of organizing the workshop wouldn't even let me audit it. She went so far as to threaten me with lifetime banishment from Broadway if I tried to get in. Understanding the ultimate power that secretaries hold to influence the course of human events in any organization, I knew better than to challenge her further.

I returned to Los Angeles, quickly followed up with a composer I'd met right before leaving for Israel, and almost immediately we co-founded Broadway on Sunset, a musical theatre development program we hosted every Monday night at Gio's, a restaurant and cabaret on Sunset Boulevard near the Strip. Each week, I line-produced and served as MC for a 90-minute show which included excerpts from new musicals, an interview with someone involved in or important to musical theatre, and news notes about shows, performers, and local productions. Of course my co-producer (aka my writing partner) and I featured *KAZOO* on nights when I interviewed the most important theatre contacts, keeping our fingers crossed that it might lead to something.

It worked. One of our interviewees, Ken Krezel, offered us space and support for a free workshop at the venue he managed, the Variety Arts Center in downtown Los Angeles. This six-story complex, built in 1923, features a Broadway-style house on the main floor and multiple performance spaces throughout. We were given the stage of the main theatre for rehearsals and the fourth-floor nightclub (which at the time displayed the original set of *The Tonight Show with Johnny Carson*) as our public venue. Each of the nine performances pulled full houses and standing ovations. With a cast that included Broadway veterans, directed and choreographed by Michael Tye-Walker – newly arrived from successful gigs directing in London's West End – it looked like *KAZOO* was on its way.

Not quite. While the show worked like gangbusters, to date it has not received another production. The composer veered off into producing other people's shows and teaching, and he chose not to keep up with the technology necessary for professional industry composers. We never had the money to hire the talent to cut a decent demo. I was a good line producer, taking care of on-site issues every Monday night, but lacked the entrepreneurial skills to raise money and promote the show to a higher level. And so even as Broadway on Sunset continued, *KAZOO*, my Three Mile Island musical, languished.

I returned to writing the political satire I'd been working on right before that bullhorn at TMI interrupted my life. I infused the material with a more specific nuclear focus and changed the name to: *AARMAGEDDON: The Living End!* I framed it as a positive look at the end of the world. Twenty years before personal computers appeared on all our desks, it told the story of an adolescent girl lost inside a computer that was programmed with the political observations and fears of her father, an aging hippie. It ultimately proposed that each of us could make a difference in the world by visualizing a better outcome to our shared human story – and taking action.

We attracted a producer, a petite blue-eyed Beverly Hills blonde of delicate demeanor, fresh out of detox for cocaine and wanting to do something with her Recovery that had nothing in common with a 12-Step program. What better environment for a calm, diverting excursion into sober living than producing a backers audition for a Broadway-intended musical?

Blinded by my desire to rush back to Israel, I refused to recognize the warning signals and plunged into action. The producer's co-dependent boyfriend provided a seemingly endless flow of money to hire a director of my choosing and a really good cast. They rented the Mayfair Theatre, a faux English music hall with great acoustics located in Santa Monica, only four blocks from the ocean. The producer flew in her potential financial "angels," a southern couple who seemed only too happy to avail themselves of her boyfriend's high-end hospitality without promising a single thing in return.

The presentation went well, with a large audience providing enthusiastic response. I narrated the script, sang chorus, and got to solo on my Marlene Dietrich/*Blue Angel*-ish song, "Only One Mile from Three Mile Island."

At the post-presentation party, I sat between the two southerners and bit my tongue as I listened to their anti-Semitic "jokes." At one point they asked me what I thought about the script. Like any optimistic writer, I said, "I think it's in good shape. There will be changes in development, of course, but I think we're pretty much there."

When these two returned to their southern manse, they informed the producer that they couldn't possibly become involved with *Aarmageddon* because, and here I quote: "The Jewgirl writer refuses to make any changes."

The project collapsed and everyone turned on me. By the time I met with the producer to protest my innocence, she was wearing dark glasses and slumping against her boyfriend. He blamed me for her going back on drugs. My manager blamed me for killing the deal and dropped me. The composer and I were already not talking, so that pretty much made it a Grand Slam.

End of the world, indeed.

Repeatedly over the coming years, I got involved in writing other shows with other partners, somehow confusing my Israeli imperative to get *KAZOO* up and running with some cosmic destiny to become an avatar of musical theatre.

LOL.

The time was not without its memorable moments. One show I wrote received a staged reading in New York directed by legendary musical theatre star Gwen Verdon (the original lead in *Sweet Charity* and former wife of Bob Fosse). Crammed with Gwen and three actors into a tiny dressing room – the only space available to rehearse a scene – she gave me a lesson in script editing I'll never forget as she cut my "un-cuttable" five-page scene down to a page-and-a-smidge.

Bob Fosse himself attended the performance, along with Broadway notables including Tony Award winners Robin Wagner (set design, *A Chorus Line*) and Jules Fisher (lighting design, almost every notable show from the 1970's and 80's). I remember nothing of what Fosse said to me in the post-show reception, only how incredibly soft his hand was as he shook mine and a single thought filled my mind: "Jerusalem!" This was Destiny Fulfilled!

Except that Fosse hated the show and wasn't shy about saying so. I can't say I blamed him. It was only the third draft of a new musical. You don't show your mother the third draft of a new musical, let alone an audience of the Broadway elite. But my 30-years-older partner felt time running out for him to make his mark and pushed for this reading before we were ready. On Broadway as in life, you only get one chance to make a first impression, and ours stank.

The collaboration fell apart within a week of the performance.

My musical theatre losing streak continued. I worked on – and lost – several more shows, an almost unheard-of run of bad luck even in the fickle world of entertainment. Each one attracted attention and praise, but each fell apart at about the workshop level – for a different reason in every case, but with the same result: the show died, taking with it years of effort and hope. Still, I persisted in the field beyond all reason.

The longer I stayed away from Israel, the more I lost focus on what I was doing, why I was doing it, and where it was all supposed to lead. Meanwhile, to support myself, I worked temp jobs for the studios, most usually Norman Lear's company (a far cry from the days when they asked my input to an on-air program) and 20th Century Fox. I used my typing speed and phone skills to under-earn, pending what I stubbornly considered my inevitable Broadway success, financial elevation, and triumphant return to Israel.

Every year, as late March approached, I tried to get something new in print about Three Mile Island. That's how I learned the hard way that the media had no interest in such a cold story. Query letters remained unanswered, spec articles rejected, others left unwritten. Slowly, I drifted away from thinking about Three Mile Island or nuclear issues or Israel or changing the world. Instead, I continued to slug it out beyond all reason with my dream of that Broadway hit.

CHAPTER 6

A CRIME OF POWER

In the mid-1980's, news began to surface about the discovery of organized, ritualized sexual abuse of toddlers at a southern California preschool. During a lull in work at a movie production office, I picked up a copy of *Time* magazine and flipped to the cover story on the case. It shook me to my core. Not only was it talking honestly about child abuse, the text expressed sympathy and empathy towards the kids. They were not ignored or minimized. Their claims were taken seriously and the underlying tone of the story was justifiable outrage at what had been done to them.

Society's new environment of believing the children who said they'd been abused (the backlash had not yet formed) gave me permission to remember incidents from my own childhood, and my subconscious started releasing memories of sexual abuse. The experiences had started so early and been so traumatic, I'd buried them in amnesia. The flood of images and emotions that came rushing out virtually incapacitated me.

To do the deep release and healing work I needed, I attended a retreat workshop for women survivors of sexual and ritual abuse. It was modeled on the work of the late Dr. Elisabeth Kubler-Ross, who's perhaps best known to the general public through Bob Fosse's use of her Five Stages of Grief (denial, anger, depression, bargaining, acceptance) in *All That Jazz*.

The irony did not escape me.

For this five-day workshop, 30 women incest survivors gathered at a yoga retreat facility in the California high desert. In the main meeting room, four mattresses on the floor provided safe, cushioned surfaces on which to do our work. Guided by five therapists and pledged to follow a thoroughly explained set of rules designed to keep us safe, we allowed ourselves to bring up the feelings we'd been working so hard to suppress. Invariably, this led to memories breaking into consciousness, which released a flood of intense emotion. We were encouraged to safely physicalize our feelings by hitting phone books with rubber hoses, saying what was previously unsayable about our experiences, and making as much noise as we needed in order to release suppressed emotions and memories.

Those of us not doing the work on mattresses partici-pated as witnesses, often being triggered into our own emotional releases. It got pretty loud in that meditation room, but for all the seeming chaos and bedlam, the flow of experience was kept tightly controlled. The therapists me-ticulously structured those five days to create a safe passage first into our feelings, then out of the pain and learned helplessness through a release that allowed for the healing of our deepest wounds. Emotionally, we were lanc-ing the deep, old infection and letting out the poisonous pus of sexual abuse and trauma.

I attended this retreat three years in a row, each time releasing major encrusted deposits of emotional excrement and clearing the way for ever-deeper healing.

The second year I went coincided with the sixth anniversary of Three Mile Island. Somewhere in the middle of raging at long-absent perpetrators and waling the shit out of a phone book, my focus shifted to Three Mile Island – and I kept screaming:

At nuclear reactors and the radioactive poisons they spew.

At the terrible destructive force of radiation on the human body.

At the Nuclear Regulatory Commission for not protecting me or even warning me in time to help myself.

At the politicians who would not listen, did not care, worked only to manage us away from panic and into complacency so they could be re-elected.

At the nuclear industry and the people in it who put money ahead of human safety and never considered their technology's toxic, deadly legacy.

At my ongoing, daily fear of cancer and the clock still ticking in the back of my brain.

For the children I would never allow myself to have.

That's when I realized how the two core issues of my life were directly related:

- Incest is defined within the politicized Recovery community as a crime of power over a child that takes a sexual form. Three Mile Island was a crime of nuclear power over our bodies that took the form of radiation exposure.
- Incest is perpetrated on helpless children by those who have positions of power and authority over

them. The nuclear industry, through its reactors, perpetrate against people who are helpless to stop them from being built and operated - meaning every child, woman, and man.

- In both instances, these perpetrations are invisible, hidden, and denied as doing or having done any harm.
- Incest perpetrators blame the victims for their fears, tell them they're overreacting, making too big a thing about it, and if they say anything, they're going to cause irreparable harm to the family and it will be *all their fault*! Politicians and pro-nukers blame those of us who raise issues against their technology as "alarmists," tell us we're "overreacting," "too emotional," we "don't understand the real issues," or we're "making too big a thing about ongoing radiation releases and safety issues," and if we continue to complain, we "risk causing irreparable harm to climate change, the economy, and the American Way of Life, and it will be *all our fault!*"
- Perpetrators have no empathy for their victims. Nuclear advocates, politicians, and business leaders in America have proven as sensitive to the nuclear issue as an incest perpetrator is to his or her victim.
- The negative impact of perpetration, sexual or nuclear, lasts forever.

After that breakthrough, I spent long hours at the workshop releasing my no-longer-repressed nuclear pain and rage, realizing the betrayal of my trust, violation of my body, processing the resulting emotions, and coming to a place of exhausted understanding.

During this era of my life, I changed my name to Libbe HaLevy, so that I was not subliminally reminded of the things that had been done to me while people called me by my original name.

Stunned by the parallel between the Three Mile Island and sexual abuse aspects of my life, I nevertheless continued to ignore nuclear information even as I "came out" once again, this time as an incest survivor. I wrote and helped produce a play on incest and recovery, *Shattered Secrets*, which ran 2-1/2 years in Los Angeles, toured California, got published, and spun off productions in Berlin, Stockholm, and around the United States.

I volunteered to work the phones for the Childhelp National Child Abuse Hotline (1-800-4-A-CHILD). The first week of training, about 15-20 well-intentioned people showed up, eager to work on the hotline. That week, the training focused on ritualistic abuse and pedophilia cults; one of the McMartin moms presented. The following week, I was the only one who turned up for the training.

I volunteered on the front lines of the hotline for over a year, taking calls originating around the country from terrified children, worried parents, suicidal adults, and perps who just wanted to jerk us around. Especially painful were the days when, after a TV talk show or news segment on child abuse aired, the Childhelp phone number was cavalierly shown up on the TV screen with no notice to the hotline… and of course, no donation from the media outlet to cover the results. We'd be swamped for days, a condition we referred to as "being Geraldo'ed" after one of the primary offenders.

Through Childhelp, in conjunction with *Shattered Secrets*, I worked with some of the McMartin families whose children had triggered that *Time* magazine cover article that so thoroughly triggered me. The operators of the preschool went on trial, and when – after a 30-month trial – the verdicts on multiple charges against the defendants came in "not guilty,"[13] I helped coordinate a press conference by McMartin parents and their supporters in front of the downtown L.A. Federal Courthouse. It seemed the combined media of the world attended in a mega-media scrum. I spoke briefly, saying in part: "Wake up, America. This is your wake-up call. We believe the children because once we WERE the children – and no one believed us." It became the sound bite *du jour* in local media and even ended up on *Sixty Minutes*.

But the tide had turned against believing victims of childhood sexual abuse. Many survivors had sued their perpetrators and won, with the courts mandating huge settlements to the victims, but those accused and found guilty hit back. From out of nowhere, a massively funded, coordinated campaign emerged pushing a brand new concept: "false memory syndrome." Basically, it insisted that we survivors were all "so-called" victims of sexual abuse, we didn't remember what we remembered, that our memories were "distorted" or coached into place by greedy, malicious, and/or incompetent therapists, and we were just a bunch of ego-tripping, attention-seeking, money-grubbing liars. Suddenly, there appeared a foundation dedicated to this "false memory" nonsense. It had the funds to fly curiously credentialed "experts" around the country to speak on TV talk shows, get interviewed by newspapers, appear in national magazine spreads, and basically cut incest survivors off at the knees... or higher.

The media – bored to tears and frustration by seven years of covering the McMartin trials[14] – lapped it up with no critical thinking whatsoever, never investigating how this new "syndrome" manifested full blown and fully funded from out of nowhere, taking no account of the fact that it was founded and supported by parents who had been sued by an adult daughter for incest. Instead, reporters and news directors welcomed it as a "new angle" on an old story. Hollywood types got on board to support the accused pre-school owners.[15] Public opinion shifted and suddenly the McMartin kids – who were now teens and eminently less appealing to the masses than they had been as toddlers – became the subject of derision, ridicule, contempt. Everyone felt free to assume they were lying.

Which led to the first joke I ever wrote:

According to supporters of "false memory syndrome," how many incest survivors does it take to screw in a lightbulb?

None – they don't need any light, nobody screwed anything, and it's all your therapist's fault.

But the situation wasn't funny. An Incest Survivor Movement, still in its infancy, crumbled under the weight of these false accusations against our lived truth. Whoever, whatever the opposition consisted of, they surmised that we survivors were not yet strong enough to stand up to their coordinated full court press. Unfortunately, they were right.

At that point, the first production of *Shattered Secrets* had closed after 2-1/2 years. A second production eliminated some dialog to insert music and choreographic movement to convey the pain of sexual abuse. It was directed by Tony™ Award winning Director/Choreographer Grover Dale, who'd been in the original *West Side Story* on Broadway. Michel Stuart, who was in the original *A Chorus*

Line and produced *Nine* on Broadway, produced it. Grover's work added a rich, unexpected dimension to the show and production time proved a lovely experience.

We opened in a small North Hollywood dance studio with great hopes, but impeccably bad timing. It was the same night as O.J. Simpson's slow speed chase, and despite holding the curtain for close to an hour, we still lost most of our audience and all of the reviewers. We never recovered from the lost momentum.

After that production closed, Michel Stuart talked to me about producing the show in its original form, developing it with actors sitting around and sharing about their personal issues, just as they did in the development phase of *A Chorus Line*. He left me a phone message about setting up a time in the next week to start planning it out. I was ecstatic. Michel was a sweetheart. We'd made a close bond with each other in the first production and I knew the experience working with him, especially in this manner, would be sublime.

The next thing I heard, Michel had been killed in a car crash on Pacific Coast Highway. Two devastating losses at one blow.[16]

I continued working within the Recovery community as a speaker and leader of writing workshops for incest survivors. I became a go-to interviewee whenever anything related to sexual abuse made the news. Once, I even debated a dead-faced rep for that foundation about "false memory" on a live news broadcast. From response I got afterwards, it was clear the newsroom staff and camera crew believed that I was telling the truth.

For a brief time, some people in Hollywood seemed interested in optioning *Shattered Secrets*[17] for film or cable, but the deal fell through. By that time, I needed to get on with my life in a way that did not find me sidetracked into activism.

For a while, that strategy worked... until it didn't.

CHAPTER 7

CHERNOBYL AND DENIAL

While immersed in recovering from childhood sexual abuse, I paid absolutely no attention to nuclear issues. Yet I couldn't seem to avoid the subject. Stray factoids related to Three Mile Island kept finding their way to me.

At a Passover Seder, I met a man who shot photos for the annual report of Babcock and Wilcox, the company that designed and built the nuclear reactors at Three Mile Island. His instructions included:

- Show the greatest possible amount of greenery.
- Shoot blue skies but no clouds, because clouds could be interpreted as radioactive emissions coming from the plant.
- Frame animals in the foreground whenever possible, with suggestions for using a cow or two placidly munching grass as cooling towers rose majestically in the background.
- Show no people.

He laughed at the manipulation of it all while admitting that the nuclear industry paid well, in full, and on time – no small matters for a freelance photographer. But he did confess that he shot everything around the reactors quickly "and then got the hell out of Dodge" for fear of radiation exposure.

I met Shelley-Anne Wooderson Martin, a former New Zealander who is a lovely storyteller and author. From her, I learned why New Zealand lamb is so expensive. It dates back to 1984, when the country went nuclear-free and banned nuclear-powered or nuclear-armed ships from using New Zealand ports or entering the country's waters.

Shelley-Anne said that the United States wasn't about to declare whether or not any of its ships had anything nuclear on them, not to any nation, let alone to a pipsqueak country like New Zealand! To its credit, the New Zealand government did not back down and refused to allow undeclared US ships to dock in their country; in 1987, it extended the nuclear ban to its air space.[18] In retaliation, the U.S. pulled an international hissy fit and imposed a 500% import tariff on New Zealand lamb. That's why the country's lamb chops are so frickin' expensive – but at least you can relax and enjoy them in the knowledge that they're as radiation-free as any meat on this planet.

At the Alliance for Survival, I'd read a book I found in their office library. It contained graphic photos taken on the ground during the days immediately after the atomic bombs fell on Hiroshima and Nagasaki – heartrending images I can never, will never forget. In this book, I learned that after those atomic bombs exploded, the only victims in the blast perimeter not affected by radiation sickness were those who ate a macrobiotic diet.

So for a while I macro'ed out and ate a lot of seaweed, grains, and miso. Until I couldn't. I just couldn't.

While not succeeding as a long-term macrobiotic, I did put myself on the equivalent of an anti-cancer protocol. I adopted as clean a diet as I could manage, buying organics, flirting with full-time vegetarianism,[19] gulping down a wide array of supplements and herbs, subjecting myself to a variety of detox regimens. I saw only holistic health practitioners. I refused x-rays whenever possible. If one proved unavoidable (e.g., a broken arm), I'd tell the tech that I thought I might be pregnant – never the case, but the only way to guarantee that I'd be given the greatest possible protection for parts of my body that didn't need to be imaged.[20] I wanted to push my life span to the farthest reaches of that cancer clock in the back of my brain, if not beyond.

On April 26, 1986, an explosion at reactor 4 at Ukraine's Chernobyl nuclear facility meant a nuke story again commanded front page news around the world. I did my best to ignore it. In the faces of friends and strangers alike, I saw nuclear fears made manifest. But I felt no empathy for them and almost scorned their concerns. I'd already lived through a nuclear disaster and did not want or need to be reminded of that experience by paying attention to this new one. I didn't have the energy to face it again and didn't have to because it wasn't in my literal backyard. I turned off the media when reports came on, walked away from conversations, did not engage, claiming what I thought was a moral high ground.

In truth, I was just as scared as everyone else, if not more so. Every mention of Chernobyl threatened to trigger my not-yet-recognized PTSD, dormant but still alive and ready to kick my butt even after all those years. I didn't feel strong enough to consider what was happening in Ukraine and its implications for the world. I just wanted the story to go away – and mainstream media, at the barest beginnings of its aversion to difficult stories that challenged generally accepted knowledge, soon complied.

But I never fully escaped reminders of the nuclear presence in our own backyards. Every time I drove south from Los Angeles to San Diego on the I-5 Freeway, I went directly past the two nuclear reactors at San Onofre Nuclear Generating Station – referred to by its acronym "SONGS," so that every time anyone protested against "SONGS," it sounded like we hated music. I'd speed up to get past it while suppressing a shudder. I always wondered why such a violent, poisonous source of energy was made to look like two impossibly over-augmented women's breasts, complete with ludicrously erect nipples. The inappropriateness of the imagery – conflating the natural source of our species' infant nourishment with radiation-poisoned energy – was either a brilliant, intentional public relations coup by nuclear strategists, or the manifestation of subliminal hatred towards all things feminine and nurturing, including Mother Earth.

Probably both.

One year, I took a Thanksgiving trip to R-Ranch in the Sierras, a timeshare trailer park cum family retreat center adjacent to Sequoia National Forest. As I stood in an endless line for communal Thanksgiving dinner, I fell into conversation with two men right behind me, both engineers who worked at the nearby Diablo Canyon nuclear facility. I shared with them my experience at Three Mile Island and its resulting impact on my life.

They laughed. As I later learned, *their* nuclear reactor had been built atop an active earthquake fault that was also a sacred Native American burial ground; has plutonium-contaminated waste with a 24,000 year half-life held in thin-shelled storage canisters prone to leaking in a saltwater environment; and that those canisters are only rated by the NRC to last for 25 years. But these men could only speak proudly of the lifestyle they'd been able to create for their families because the nuclear industry paid so well.

In the late 90's a dear friend, actress Joan Hotchkis, invited me to join her and a few others at a private fundraising event with Dr. Helen Caldicott. Joan had starred as William Windom's wife in the series *My World and Welcome To It*; as Jack Klugman's girlfriend on TV's *The Odd Couple*; and the mother in the film *Ode to Billie Joe*. When she hit 40 and Hollywood roles dried up, she moved into performance art, writing and performing award-winning shows.

I produced her 1996-97 hit one-woman performance, *Elements of Flesh: or Screwing Saved My Ass. Elements* was years if not decades ahead of its time, dealing with issues of aging and sexuality before Boomers realized that this meant us. Audiences went wild over the content, which broke the societal taboo against a mature woman talking frankly about her sex life, let alone in such an elegant, adult way. As a performer, Joan was an object lesson in how to keep a show unique and fresh, organic and real, every performance. Closing night, the line was out the door. Leonard Nimoy showed up with his new wife, hoping for standby tickets. Of course, I ushered him in; who could deny Spock?

A final vision of Joan from the show: as a black-and-white home movie montage of her ever-earlier years played in the background, lights slowly came up on her reclining on a bed, back to the audience, looking coyly over her shoulder. She was naked except for an exquisite Chinese silk robe that draped over one shoulder and fell away to half-cover her ass, leaving one bare cheek in full view.

My job was to drape the robe and tuck it into her ass crack.[21]

We should all look so good at 68.

When Joan invited me to hear Dr. Caldicott speak, I jumped at the chance. It was her interview in *LA Weekly* that first alerted me to the health risks I faced following Three Mile Island. Out of everything I'd read or heard since, Dr. Caldicott was the only one who'd stated the hard truth. I'd never heard her speak, either in the media or in person, so I eagerly anticipated the evening.

We drove to a lavish Santa Monica mansion where entertainment industry celebrities, movers, and shakers mingled while awaiting her talk. I introduced myself to Dr. Caldicott as having been at Three Mile Island... and watched her face change to an expression of concern. It was the first acknowledgement I'd received from anyone that showed they understood exactly what my experience meant.

And that's the last I remember of the meeting – not a word she said, the response from the audience, even the name of the book she was promoting. When Joan offered to buy me a copy and have it autographed, I declined. I didn't want that thing anywhere near my life. As we drove back to Joan's home, I maintained complete silence. She asked me in with the others to discuss the evening, but I begged off, claiming tiredness and a long drive home.

I got in my car, drove about three car lengths, pulled over to the curb and sat there, unable to move, unable to think, frozen the exact same way I'd been frozen in front of that bathroom mirror more than two decades before. Catatonic, dissociative, numb – I couldn't think of words to describe my state. Indeed, I could not think in words at all. Despite the time, the distance, and the emotional work I'd done, that primal fear from Three Mile Island roared back and froze me where I sat.

After about 15 minutes of this, I realized I needed to do something, so I forced myself out of the car to knock on Joan's door. When she saw me, I blurted out what had happened and she drew me into a compassionate hug. I broke down, sobbing. She and the others sat with me as I babbled out a disjointed retelling of my TMI experience, something I'd not talked about outside of a therapeutic environment for years. After almost two hours, I'd dispelled enough of my tension and fear to be able to drive home.

The PTSD hadn't gone away; it simply went into hibernation, waiting for a recognizable jolt from the outside world to launch it back into full attack mode. After seeing Dr. Caldicott's instantaneous understanding and compassion, I felt like I lived in an alternate reality again, somehow separate from the rest of the world.

Recognizing nuclear's power to terrify me from within, I spent the next weeks doing everything I could to push that genie back into the bottle – food, compulsive reading, excess sleep, hikes in nature with the dogs, too many DVDs. I fought the depression by stuffing it down as far as I could. I wanted to go back to living my life in the land of nuclear denial.

Made it, too. At least, for a little while…

CHAPTER 8

HEALTH: NUCLEAR'S HIDDEN EROSION

Time passed, and to my great relief, the cancer clock in the back of my brain ran down its full 15 years with no leukemia or hard tumors. For some reason, I interpreted Dr. Caldicott's timeline as meaning that if I survived 15 years without cancer, I'd have earned a Get Out of (cancer) Jail Free card and the danger would be over.[22] Yes, my hair did gray out at a shockingly early age – according to Dr. Caldicott, one of the minor side effects of exposure to low level radiation. But I had no vanity about it, just a vague sense of accomplishment because I seemed to have ducked the nuclear bullet with only this one cosmetic change.

But in my mid-40's, I began to feel tired most of the time. Pervasive fatigue interfered with my ability to live the life I wanted. I figured this was a side effect of menopause, just the machinery running down, even as I sensed that I was too young to feel this old. I didn't have health insurance at the time, so running to doctors, getting tests, and buying meds if prescribed was pretty much out of the question. As a result, I surrendered to the thought that this was just what it meant to get older and I'd have to learn to live with it.[23]

I accommodated my ever-decreasing energy with frequent naps, a shortened work schedule, and a reluctant refusal to go to events I wanted to attend because I knew that if I went, I'd stress myself back into fatigue, and the exhaustion would last for days. Eventually, I developed killer insomnia that left me more tired in the mornings than when I'd gone to bed. I felt trapped in a body that had forgotten how to sleep, how to rest.

At the suggestion of an acupuncturist friend who'd struggled with her own issues of insomnia and exhaustion, I read *Adrenal Fatigue: The 21st Century Stress Syndrome* by James Wilson. From it, I learned that adrenal problems can be created by stress, which triggers the glands into a fight or flight response. Back in cave days, this biochemical means of generating emergency energy helped us defend against a marauding tribe or saber-toothed tiger. Afterwards, assuming the emergency had passed, the adrenalin subsided and adrenal glands reset to their normal level.

These glands were never meant to be continuously stressed the way they are by modern life. Multiple sustained triggering events in a day, every day (think: traffic) mean the adrenal glands never have a chance to fully recover before being forced into action again and again. As a result, they wear down and deplete to exhaustion, resulting in severe lack of energy, the aforementioned insomnia, a foggy brain, and dozens of other symptoms, none of them good, many of which I had.

This information took a deeper meaning for me when I read that adrenal fatigue can be precipitated by a single major stress event. The book's medically-based self-diagnostic quiz asked: "When is the last time you remember feeling completely well?"

It shocked me to realize that I hadn't felt completely healthy for 30 years – since right before Three Mile Island. Apparently, the months of raging post-traumatic stress set me up for decades of undiagnosed, ever-decreasing adrenal function that led to my current state of exhaustion.

Armed with this new information, I researched holistic options to heal my overstressed adrenals. Fortunately, my dear friend as well as acupuncturist/herbalist, Dr. Diane Sandler,[24] had just completed advanced training on adrenal issues. Starting with blood work to guide her recommendations, she designed a specific protocol meant to provide healing. On a daily basis, I took pills, capsules, creams, and a special nutritional powder in my smoothies; made my diet gluten-free, food-combined, and as alkaline as possible; tried to go to bed by 10 p.m. every night (a real toughie); and turned down any activity that would not end long before 8 p.m. so as to not stress myself into insomnia. I learned to no longer push myself through fatigue, but to recognize its warning signs and rest. Over time, my adrenals and I recovered enough that I can live a more robust life, as long as I respect certain limits.

I had gone back to school, the University of Santa Monica, to receive a Masters Degree in Spiritual Psychology in 2001.[25] After graduation, I used those skills to become certified as a Life and Business Coach. I developed a private clientele, subcontracted to a major international coaching firm, and did some freelance writing on the side, mostly website copy for small businesses. My clients included stage and screen legend Julie Andrews, for whom I facilitated a business retreat; New York Times bestselling author Emma Walton Hamilton; and Dr.

Michael Rabinoff, a first-time author whose book on smoking cessation has been endorsed by the Dalai Lama.

For a while, I continued chasing the Broadway dream through several more failed projects. The most promising one was *Now, Voyager: The Musical,* based on the same source material as the beloved Bette Davis movie. I framed it as the story of a woman who breaks the cycle of abuse and passes healing on to the next generation, cleverly disguised as an ugly duckling finds love. This show represented 12 years of my writing life, working with partners so closely attuned that we operated like three lobes of the same brain.[26]

The show was accepted for the prestigious, Steven Schwartz-led ASCAP/Disney Musical Theatre Workshop, where we presented concert readings of two excerpts to a discerning audience that did not, unfortunately, include Mr. Schwartz. That year, he was in pre-Broadway rewrites on what would become his most famous hit, *Wicked.* As a result, the workshop was left in the hands of a writer who was in the process of experiencing two simultaneous Broadway flops. Understandably, this made him extremely bitter – and he vented his spleen on our show, lashing out at us in front of the audience, cueing his co-panelists to use us for comedic target practice, which they did.

Afterwards, audience members, including top pros, took us aside and told us that the show they'd seen us present and the one he was critiquing were two entirely different musicals. Yet despite how unfair his flaming attack had been, he'd done his dirt. This ASCAP opportunity, which often saw the featured shows receiving immediate offers of further readings, workshops, and even productions, led absolutely nowhere.

Ultimately, obscure problems sank this highly promising show – and when *Now, Voyager* died, it truly broke my heart. I did pursue writing one more original musical, this one set in the world of high profile seminar leaders. I attracted a truly fine, professional, accomplished composer, Jay Gruska, as a partner. But my heart wasn't in it. Even at its best, when we succeeded in cranking out two really good songs, I felt like I was just marking time.[27]

I'd grown far enough away from Three Mile Island that the 30th anniversary in 2009 passed without my notice. I never moved back to Israel, letting myself get sucked into the energetic miasma of America and convincing myself that I was living a rich, fulfilling life. I never looked at nuclear energy as existing or being a factor in anyone's life, let alone mine. I'd lulled myself into the Great American State of Complacency.

But when I looked at all I'd not accomplished after so many promising beginnings, I felt that in some important way, I was a failure.

And then, Fukushima.

CHAPTER 9

FUKUSHIMA: THE SECOND MULE KICK

March 11, 2011. A 9.0 earthquake hits off the northeast coast of Japan. The resulting 45-foot tsunami inundates the land. Unprecedented devastation to cities follows, with loss of human life in the tens of thousands and the entire northeast coast of Japan reeling from nature's violent assault – a terrifying scenario.

I followed the events on social media, catching updated posts and horrifying videos, clicking on links, joining the rest of the world as we bore online, real-time witness to the destruction.

Then came word of damage to a nuclear facility on the Japanese coast. Not one but three nuclear reactors flooded.[28] Cooling systems destroyed. Back-up generators for emergency cooling systems destroyed. Radiation being released in untold amounts.[29] Reactors overheating and meltdowns in progress in Units 1, 2 and 3, with the growing threat of a nuclear explosion. Only the efforts of "The Fukushima 50,"[30] a small cadre of technicians led by plant manager Masao Yoshida, prevented the disaster from growing even worse. They stayed on site at Fukushima Daiichi to fight the meltdowns despite the danger and lack of supplies. Only they stood between what was happening at the reactors and the possible devastation of our entire ecosphere.[31]

Officials from facility operator Tokyo Electric Power Company (TEPCO) either hadn't a clue or flat-out lied about the extent of the damage, denying the existence of "meltdowns"[32] even to Japanese Prime Minister Naoto Kan, pretending it wasn't as bad as it was, reassuring the public away from panic by denial and PR manipulation. Meanwhile, unannounced and invisible, a radiation plume spewed out from the demolished reactors.[33]

The plume's first inadvertent victims were sailors on the aircraft carrier USS Ronald Reagan, who were performing an humanitarian aid mission to the tsunami-ravaged area and never given warning of the radiation danger by TEPCO. As a result, the sailors wore no protective gear while working on the deck and were exposed to the most intense of the radiation release. Even when the captain became aware of the problem and tried to move his ship out of the plume, without information from TEPCO or the Japanese government, the Reagan retreated but remained in the hot spot of the plume's trajectory. (USS Reagan sailors have since become seriously ill: some have died; had limbs amputated; autoimmune diseases are rampant; there have been miscarriages; and birth defects found in babies exposed *in utero* include withered limbs. This happened to an adult population that was at the peak of health before Fukushima. And yes, there is now a billion-dollar lawsuit against TEPCO on behalf of the sailors.[34])

From my first awareness of this nuclear disaster, the fear programmed into me by Three Mile Island roared back to life in all its PTSD glory. I slept fitfully with the computer next to my bed. Every time I awoke, I obsessively Googled for the latest information. Each piece of worsening news felt personal, invasive, assaultive. It triggered in me a desperate need to communicate to others what I already understood about this disaster: that ultimately, we could be facing a global endgame.

The bad news continued. Plutonium was reportedly found more than a kilometer from the site, presumably from one of the hydrogen explosions that blew apart fuel rods. With no power to maintain the cooling system, the remaining fuel rods risked heating up to a point where they could trigger an atomic explosion, like an on-site A-bomb – referred to in minimizing nuke-speak as "a re-criticality event." Emergency cooling water continually sprayed on the ruins by the Fukushima 50 kept the reactors below recriticality, but the highly radioactive sea water that resulted drained into the ground and from there into the Pacific Ocean. As radioactive water spread invisibly through the sea, prevailing winds blew the airborne radiation plume east, away from Japan and towards the west coast of North America.

I live in southern California, directly in the path of the radiation plume. I'd already learned the hard way the dangers of direct exposure to a radiation release. At Three Mile Island, the day after the accident, I'd walked over a mile to Middletown, ignorant of what I was exposing myself to and oblivious to the radiological implications. I never considered the danger because, at the time, our government officials (Your Tax Dollars at Work!) would not acknowledge that anything dangerous was happening. My walk into Middletown took place after radiation had already been released from TMI into the atmosphere. Then I stood outside for almost an hour, exposed and ignorant, waiting for a bus. That night, Jeanne and I stood outside at the Middletown bus stop waiting for Jim to pick us up, exposing ourselves yet again.

Only ten days later, I browbeat that photographer into driving us to the reactor and snapping pictures as I posed in all my wrongheaded arrogance. In hindsight, I alternately want to smack that young woman upside the head for her stupidity and congratulate her on an indelible branding photo (see: book cover). At the time, however, considering the additional radiation exposure, I dismissed any fears with the thought, "In for a penny, in for a pound." As far as I knew, I'd already absorbed a deadly dose, so I figured a little more wouldn't make any difference.

Ignorance of this sort is not bliss; it's a dangerous form of denial, with potential consequences reaching far into the future.

With the Fukushima radiation plume predicted to hit the U.S. west coast eight days after the disaster began, I changed behavior to atone for my earlier TMI ignorance. I resisted stepping outside of my house if I could help it. I kept my doors and windows closed, my dog inside except for absolutely necessary walks, turned up my HEPA air filters to the max. When I couldn't avoid going out, I put a scarf over my mouth and nose. I joked with vendors at the farmer's market that I was sick, saying, "You don't want what I have and I don't want what you have." Back home, I washed my scarf with the garden hose and left it outside with my shoes and jacket for fear of contaminating my home with radioactive particles.

My appetite for information continued to prove insatiable, and the Internet fed it. Facebook provided an ongoing flow of links to heartrending information. YouTube videos showed Japanese people struggling with dignity in the face of unspeakable tragedy – black waters rushing inexorably forward, swallowing streets, cars, people, washing high rise buildings away. I linked to feeds from the New York Times, Japanese newspapers, activist groups, desperate posts from people in Japan dealing directly with the consequences. I gleaned facts and factoids that added to a terrible picture of destruction that threatened at any moment to become catastrophically worse.

This online info-stream proved especially important because around five days after the disaster began, all mainstream media references to "the radiation plume will hit North America in eight days" vanished. Just POOF! and gone. Then I watched with growing disbelief as first broadcast TV and commercial radio, then newspapers and even NPR downplayed Fukushima. The facility's operators, the Japanese government, and our government glossed over the details, and reporters did not dig into it. Within days, the story grew cold and Fukushima as good as disappeared from the news cycle.

I knew from my experience as an activist on sexual abuse issues that when reporters or their editors grow weary of a story – or it runs counter to powerful, moneyed interests – they either ignore it, downplay it, spin it, attack it, or find odd human interest angles to write about instead of hard news and analysis. All those tactics seemed in play at Fukushima, the scattershot suppression of information rushed into place in record time by vested interests with powerful media allies. As a result, Fukushima faded away from public consciousness.

Except Fukushima was still happening. The plume was still advancing. Online sources provided news stories from international sites that followed the story closely and more honestly. I morphed my Facebook page into Me-stream media, an ongoing information source on Fukushima and its consequences... whether you wanted to hear it or not.

Alas, many of my "friends" did not.

I really didn't care.

On Sunday, March 13, just two days after the earthquake and tsunami, I was scheduled to record a story for my weekly storytelling group's podcast. I'd chosen and rehearsed a sweet, nostalgic tale about re-meeting my first boyfriend after 30 years. It had already been published in the anthology, *The Story Salon Big Book of Stories*.

But a few hours before airtime, over brunch with a friend, I kept going on and on about the nuclear situation in Japan. In passing, I mentioned the storytelling podcast. He said, "You'll be talking about what's going on in Japan, right?" I started to say "No," but then it hit me: there was no other story I could possibly tell.

The program producers always urged us to tell our story – "Let your freak flag fly!" – even if it was something that happened on the way to our weekly performances. So that afternoon, I let them know I'd changed what I was going to say. I proceeded to record a raw, passionate, unrehearsed plea for nuclear sanity, including large portions of my personal experience at Three Mile Island.

When the recording session ended, one of the other podcast participants rushed up. Carl Koslovski worked at *Pasadena Weekly* and asked if my story had appeared anywhere in print. I told him it hadn't been seen or heard in 32 years, not since that first *LA Weekly* article and the *LA Times* op-ed. He quickly contacted his editor on my behalf and ten days later, my article on Fukushima appeared in the paper. Meanwhile, I again told the tale, this time to a live audience at our regular weekly storytelling gig. People appeared moved, shocked, and afraid, but lacked the context to understand it further. Many avoided me afterwards, but others came up, thanked me for the information, and asked if there was anything they could or should do.

As yet, I did not have a good answer, but told them I would find one and get back to them.

Driving home, I caught a few minutes of *The Story with Dick Gordon* on NPR and heard the program's standing offer to contact them with our stories. I dashed off an email that night about my experience at Three Mile Island and the deadly threat of Fukushima. The following Monday, Dick Gordon read the email of my story on *The Story*.

I continued to speak out wherever and whenever I could: during my turns at the storytelling group, to vendors at the farmer's market, while standing in line at Trader Joe's, the library, at networking groups supposedly focused on my coaching/writing career – anywhere I could entice or entrap someone into listening, whether they wanted the information or not. My compulsion to talk about Fukushima stuck in overdrive.

My friends initially proved tolerant, but some acquaintances became progressively less amused. Thankfully, through the stream of information on Facebook, I discovered nuclear activists – those who were new like me as well as seasoned veterans with decades of anti-nuclear experience. I devoured their posts, hit the "Like" button, friended them, and started sharing my own concerns, grateful to finally be in a community that could hear me and understood. Their ever-increasing number of posts turned my personal/professional Facebook page into a clearinghouse for the latest nuclear information, my own AP/UPI news feed on all things nuclear. I lost a lot of casual and business "friends" with that switch, but after Fukushima, cute kitty videos and seminar promos just didn't cut it for me.

I wrote emails to editors demanding better coverage from mainstream media and filled in the information holes of whatever articles they'd published. I posted comments online in response to articles on the *New York Times* and *Los Angeles Times* websites, then branched off into *Huffington Post*, news services, TV networks, my local NPR affiliate. I conducted a running debate with the *New York Times* Tokyo Bureau Chief to label Fukushima's triple meltdown as "the world's *worst* nuclear disaster," not "the worst *since* Chernobyl."[35] I felt frantic to do something, anything to make a difference... or at least not feel so helpless.

To give myself some sense of control over Fukushima's possible consequences on my health, I researched holistic detox treatments, supplements, and radiation-protection protocols to add to the little I already knew. I discovered a video on the benefits of using clay to detoxify and eventually started taking liquid zeolite drops to remove possible radiation and heavy metals from my body.[36] When I re-learned the anti-radiation benefits of a macrobiotic diet after Hiroshima, I immediately went to Whole Foods and bought out their supply of organic miso, a fermented soybean paste that's a cornerstone of the diet. I moved fast to stock up because I understood that the only guarantee of "clean" food was to grab whatever had been produced, packaged, and shipped before March 11, 2011. Weeks later, it surprised me to find these products still on the shelves. Apparently, I was among the few who understood the dangers we faced because of Fukushima and felt a compulsion to stockpile the only guaranteed radiation-free products.

Fukushima took over my life. I had a hard time concentrating on anything else. Nothing seemed as important as this unfolding disaster. I felt as though I were living in a science fiction book, during an era referred to as "The time when everything had already irrevocably changed, only the people were too ignorant, arrogant, or manipulated to realize it. So they behaved as though everything was the same until the difference was impossible to ignore… and by then it was too late."

Audiences at the storytelling group repeatedly found themselves on the receiving end of depressing nuclear updates, which did not sit well with certain influential members, and the official atmosphere towards me grew chilly. Braver attendees would sidle up to me afterwards to quietly ask, "How bad is it? Should I be doing something? Is there anything I *can* do?" They shared a learned helplessness on all matters nuclear, and while they didn't trust mainstream media's reassurances that everything was okay, they didn't know where to turn for advice.

I became their default source. Privately, I shared the best information I had gleaned, our few minutes of conversation inadequate to convey the scope of the problem, the magnitude of the danger, the depth of need for taking self-preservation steps, and what those steps might be.[37]

Except for those infrequent questions and the anti-nuclear individuals I found and messaged with on Facebook, I was alone with my fears. I wandered through life with a sense of impending doom, convinced that in my immediate world, only I could see what was happening, the danger to us all. When I walked the dog on a local fire road or in nearby mountains, I regularly teared up at the preciousness, the beauty, the fragility of life, and how we had taken its continuance for granted. With the Fukushima disaster ongoing, uncontrolled and running in the background of the entire planet, how could people act as if life itself had not been changed forever?

Answer: Because they did not know, or if they knew, they did not understand, or if they understood, they did not care. The mainstream media blackout successfully dulled the story to a vague past tense. Fukushima was over, wasn't it?

Absolutely not. In the history of the world, as it may one day be understood, this disaster that was going to change everything had only just begun...

As was the part I was about to play in it.

CHAPTER 10

I CAN'T *NOT* DO IT

On April 26, 2011, the 25th anniversary of Chernobyl, I attended a showing of *The China Syndrome* sponsored by the Alliance for Survival. Suddenly, I found myself in a room with other anti-nuclear activists, engaging in The Conversation. I wasn't alone! Huzzah!

Yet the audience proved disappointingly small, those present representing the ragged remnants of a once-enormous movement. I'd expected throngs at this event, but those in attendance numbered maybe a few dozen people, no more, and only a handful were under 50 years of age.

Where were all the other anti-nuclear activists?

The evening featured a moving speech by Natalie Love-Koteva. As a seven-year-old child in Romania, she lived downwind of Chernobyl when it exploded. The Russian government, of course, released no relevant information on the disaster, so her family took no protective measures. In her early teen years, she developed the first recorded case of post-Chernobyl thyroid disease.

Now a U.S. citizen and a successful physical therapist in Los Angeles, she was working with Physicians for Social Responsibility. Natalie spoke with powerful understatement of the problems created by exposure to low level radiation such as she experienced after Chernobyl.

That night, I learned not only about Fukushima and Chernobyl but of the dangers we face here in the US from aging nuclear reactors. The most immediate threat came from the 104 nuclear reactors then on line, 23 of them the exact same GE Mark I or II reactor model still spewing radiation at Fukushima. Nuclear reactors were built to last only 40 years and then be decommissioned. That's because constant bombardment by radiation from the nuclear reaction renders each reactor's metal and concrete parts progressively more structurally compromised, or "embrittled," as they age, thus more prone to dangerous breakdowns.

But the owner-operators of two-thirds of American reactors have already applied for and received 20-year license extensions from the Nuclear Regulatory Commission (NRC), which was referred to at this meeting as the "Nuclear Rubberstamp Commission" for its unrelenting compliance with nuclear industry requests.

There have been accidents at American nuclear facilities for years, including:

- regular radiation releases of tritium – radioactive hydrogen – into the groundwater;
- "allowable" amounts of radiation released into air and water. These are arbitrary levels set by the NRC, seemingly to reassure the public and cover political asses, despite the fact these levels do not jibe with

science, which states that ANY exposure to radiation is cumulative and bad for your health;[38]

- Water used to cool the nuclear reactors is released into the lakes, rivers, and local areas of the ocean at temperatures up to 20 degrees higher than at intake, creating ecology-altering heating increases that endanger the aquatic food chain from plankton on up;
- regularly occurring accidents, fires, and "hot shutdowns" – slamming on the brakes while running at full power -- at reactors around the country, caused by anything from equipment failure to operator errors and beyond.

Everything I heard at the meeting shocked me, infuriated me, seemed enormously important… and I'd not heard any of it before. How was that possible?

Looking around the meager gathering, I realized that most of these people had been involved in anti-nuclear activism since Three Mile Island or even before. They spoke of other organizations and activists with a familiarity born of decades of shared work. They rattled off details of terror and error with alarming ease. None of this was news to them. They knew their stuff.

But they had failed to get their story out into the world in such a way that it reached me.

Admittedly, I'd fought nuclear awareness after TMI, but there were still times when I could have been made aware of the issues, if only because it cost me personal energy to ignore them. But except for the spurt of articles after Chernobyl and Dr. Caldicott's talk, for more than 30 years since TMI coverage faded, I'd heard nothing serious about anything nuclear.

Perhaps the fault lay with the activists, who had failed to effectively communicate their justifiable concerns to the media and from there to the general public.

Maybe the media was permanently tone deaf on the issues and ignored them.

Maybe I was so walled off and maintained such an iron-clad denial system that I'd missed what was being said and written.

Whatever the reason, other than a few stray bits and pieces, I remember hearing nothing about nuclear issues for 32 years.

If word about nuclear perils wasn't getting out after Fukushima, with the disaster still ongoing and no end in sight, what was it going to take to bring the dangers to people's awareness? If the populace didn't understand the threat posed by aging, leaking nuclear reactors, and the need to take action to shut them down, what would it take to wake them up – other than another sudden, life-threatening nuclear "Oops!" happening in their own back yards, by which time it would be too late? Didn't they know what nuclear radiation did to the human body? Didn't they realize the forever-ness of the threat to life itself?

The answer, of course, is no. They did not know because after the Cold War, with the rise of the commercial nuclear energy industry, the potentially frightening atomic truths got scrubbed from public education and national discourse. Indeed, the word "atomic" – as in "atomic bomb" – generated so much fear that the industry changed its go-to word to "nuclear." We were lulled into a false sense of security – not only to ignore "that little radioactive man behind the nuclear curtain," but to never see that curtain or worry about what was behind it in the first place.

I lived with a horrible conflict, feeling like Cassandra trying to warn a world that obviously didn't want to listen. My paying work suffered, I isolated from friends, glued myself to the computer for the latest news, read, posted, wept, and prayed – not unlike my behavior after Three Mile Island, except back then we didn't have the Internet and I wasn't big on prayer. The anti-nuclear movement, such as it was, needed some kind of media campaign. But I was just one person, what could I do? And before I could even consider becoming more active, I needed to find some way to sustain myself in the full upright emotional position in the face of all that I was learning or I'd never be able to spit in the nuclear devil's eye.

The single answer to both problems came from a surprising, invisible source, and again changed my life.

CHAPTER 11

WELCOME TO *NUCLEAR HOTSEAT*

Three months after Fukushima began, feeling emotionally exhausted and mired in despair, I went on a personal retreat to Sequoia National Forest. I try to get to this magnificent piece of Earth twice a year to unplug completely. I camp off grid with no digital connection and no agenda other than sleep, meditation, journaling, walks with the dog and – most importantly – taking time to hear myself think. I sit alone for hours, not another human being within sight or sound, absorbing the aching purity of nature-as-nature-intended.

This year, I spent my time wondering how much longer it would be safe for any of us to sit outside and enjoy the profound beauty of such unmolested natural wonders.

Through online reading, I'd learned that at Fukushima, hot particles of plutonium and cesium had been blasted into the upper atmosphere, where they entered the jet stream and remained in circulation around the globe. (Indeed, leftover radioactive particles from the bombs at Hiroshima, Nagasaki, and 2,121 aboveground nuclear tests still float around in the jet stream as well.) Humidity in the upper atmosphere needs particulate matter in order to form drops, and so bring these particles to earth inside rain or snow. If there's a radioactive patch of the jet stream overhead and raindrops form around hot particles, those water droplets bring radiation down to earth in what is termed a "rain-out." This phenomenon explains how post-Fukushima radiation spikes were found in such diverse and unexpected areas as St. Louis, Oklahoma, North Carolina, New England, Sweden, and Brazil. A check of the weather showed that these spikes happened in conjunction with rain or snow.[39]

I looked around my isolated campsite at the remaining snow drifts and wondered: has radiation landed here already, to be concentrated in the soil as the snow melts? Am I surrounded by the end result of a nuclear rain-out? Have I gone in search of peace only to encounter the guarantor of my destruction? Is this place safe? Is anywhere on the planet still safe? Or have we really done it – have we finally, irrevocably destroyed the Earth as a habitat for human life?

I fell into a deep, inconsolable grief, truly believing that life as we'd known it was over. I meditated, wept, apologized to the trees and the planet, stared wordlessly into the exquisite view, my journal untouched, my heart on the ground.

Then, as though a Voice were speaking directly into my right ear, I heard the words, "You will do your first podcast this Tuesday."

Excuse me?

"You will do your first podcast this Tuesday."

Now, let me be clear: I do not claim to be either clairaudient or schizophrenic. I know the difference between hearing something with my ears and the inner impulse to language that comes when I tap into my creativity. This unseen Voice was entirely different, more like something from the spiritual plane.

So of course, I debated it:

ME: I don't know how to do a podcast.

VOICE: You'll learn.

ME: What kind of a podcast...?

VOICE: Duh !

ME: But I don't know enough about nuclear things...

VOICE: You'll learn.

ME: But who am *I* to –

VOICE: Who are you *not* to?

ME: But –

VOICE: (Getting testy) If you don't do your first podcast this Tuesday, you will regret it for the rest of your life!

That stopped me. I learned a long time ago that we don't regret the things we do, only the things we don't do. I've worked hard at having the fewest possible regrets in my life, which goes a long way towards explaining the ADHD nature of my resume. If anything, I've grown to fear loss of unique experience far more than immersion in difficult situations, even with their potential for mortifying levels of embarrassment.

So though I still struggled with a great reluctance and refused to commit, I figured there was a good chance I would do my first podcast that Tuesday.

Monday morning, freshly back from Sequoia, I posted a single status update on Facebook. I said that I was thinking about doing a podcast on nuclear issues but wasn't sure if this was something people wanted, so if anyone was willing to engage in a conversation about Fukushima with me on Tuesday at 4 pm, contact me for the conference call number and PIN code. I figured that even if anyone saw my post, no one would respond and I'd be off the hook with that unseen Voice.

Thus it shocked me when two – count them! Two! – people responded, one of whom I didn't even know. Such was my first experience of social media's invisible reach.

When they called in, I had no script prepared. I simply talked, spewing off the top of my head thoughts and observations I'd gleaned from my personal experience at Three Mile Island, Cold War stories about radiation threat, what I'd learned online since Fukushima. Then I asked them if they thought my doing a weekly podcast on the stuff I'd been talking about sounded like a good idea. They both responded with an enthusiastic yes – a 100% approval rating! Their encouragement gave me the reassurance I needed, and on that day, Tuesday, June 14, 2011, *Nuclear Hotseat* was born.

I figured I'd do one show a week until I got tired of it.

The early programs were… let's be kind and say, "awkward." I kept to Tuesdays at 4 pm Pacific to go live over a conference line, with guests and call-ins. During the week, I compiled articles and links from my online searches into a document file as source for a news report. These I'd print out and use in the olde rip-and-read news format I'd learned in college radio-TV classes and at WPGU. Each show included an holistic healing or radiation protection tip, based on my own explorations with diet and supplements.

My gaffes in these first shows were legion, most notably in my mangled pronunciation of Japanese place names. For interviewees, I had only the few contacts I'd made at the

Alliance for Survival session, plus people I asked after I read their posts online. Most never bothered to respond to my request for an interview. Of the few who did agree, when the time came, many were no-shows. The online platform I used for the call played awful sub-Muzak in the background when I was the only one on the line. To avoid it, I'd beg one of those two initial callers to call in, even if they didn't listen.[40] In extremis, I had the bad manners to ask my interviewee to stay on the line beyond their interview time.[41]

When I had a guest on the line and said, "Let's open it up for questions," the silence that usually followed demonstrated just how much reach my show did not have. It got so I'd give a couple of questions to that original listener I'd harassed into being on the line, just to save face.

The interviews themselves were often an exercise in extreme naiveté. During one with retired nuclear engineer Ernest Goitein – he came over to the anti-nuclear side a long time ago – I argued that the Nuclear Regulatory Commission was really doing a good job.[42]

In short: I was a typical novice podcaster, struggling to find her voice, format, and balance. But the program served a greater function. I could not take in all this awful, toxic information without having a way to get it out. *Nuclear Hotseat* from the first helped me turn my pain, depression, and sense of powerlessness into action. For the third time in my life, I experienced the healing power of activism as I forged ahead with the program, no matter the challenges.

Early on, I read the news straight. But as is my nature, before long I started making off-the-cuff sarcastic comments about the stories, pointing out languaging tricks or blatant omissions used by the nuclear industry to manipulate public awareness. At first, I edited these bits of snark out before posting the show because, let's face it, "This is nuclear! It's serious! I can't be making jokes about it!"

As the weeks passed, these comments grew so rapidly in number that I came to consider what I was doing a form of anti-nuclear Tourette's. Eventually, a week came when I got tired of all that editing and let a few sneak by.

That's when I started getting reactions on social media, all positive, and more people began listening and sharing the link. They said they appreciated my sense of humor because, let's face it, "This is nuclear! It's serious! Thank you for making jokes about it!"

Their responses freed me up. I began incorporating everything I'd learned in my years of theatre, broadcasting, storytelling, and marketing training to entice people to pay attention to things they didn't necessarily want to know about. Puns, wordplay, funny voices, sound effects, groans, self-sung snippets of Broadway songs, and ditties of my own creation – this un-mainstream-media delivery helped provide attitude along with the stories. The more I played around with it, the more people seemed to like it. Jon Stewart of *The Daily Show* was my role model and hero.

Interviews, however, I always conducted straight. These were deep dives into specific issues, as well as my claim to credibility and the reason why experienced activists found it worth their time to listen.

Tech proved a nightmare. I have no intuitive understanding of the digital world, so everything I learned about producing audio on my computer and posting online was done one URL, one click at a time. I'd been producing the show for two months before I learned it wasn't technically a podcast, just a conference call I posted a link to once a week on Facebook. A long tutoring session with one of my service providers taught me how to create an rss feed, hook it up to iTunes, and TA DA! It was a real podcast! And iTunes became my first distribution network.

Despite all the frustrations, I persisted. Indeed, I couldn't *not* do it. From my previous activist work, I knew that this was part of what our side needed: its own information arm, promoting anti-nuclear news, ideas, and voices that weren't getting out. I didn't waste time on the show debating the "need" for nuclear energy. I followed legendary newsman Edward R. Murrow's lead. When challenged about using his *See It Now* program on CBS to go after Sen. Joseph McCarthy and the House Un-American Activities Committee, Murrow said, "I simply cannot accept that there are, on every story, two equal and logical sides to an argument."[43]

In other words, if something is categorically, unambiguously wrong, don't go out of your way to find someone to debate that it's right. This was podcasting, not broadcasting, and they killed off the Fairness Doctrine long ago.[44]

I also cherished H. L. Menken's famous statement about the true purpose of journalism: "To comfort the afflicted and afflict the comfortable."

It became my goal to tell the untold truths about nuclear that get buried under the industry's spin, the government's compromises, and the media's inattentiveness. The show represents what is now called advocacy journalism – reporting with a clearly stated purpose and perspective, but without resorting to exaggeration or misrepresentation of the facts. From the start, *Nuclear Hotseat*'s non-negotiable premise was and remains that there is no sane justification for nuclear reactors.[45]

Within those parameters, I do not exaggerate the truth of the information I glean from the world's media, and I make certain that my sources are credible. I frame this information to be as powerful as possible and do not allow for a contradictory position. No debating the "merits" of nuclear energy allowed; on my show, there are none.

I keep the language and information flow accessible to someone who knows nothing and wants to know something, as well as those who know something and want to know a little bit more. Jargon is the death of honest communications – a fact well known to nuclear industry PR flacks – and I do everything in my power to avoid it. I also keep things "clean." No George Carlin "Seven Words You Can't Say on Television (or Radio)" to give the FCC the opportunity to hassle me. Not that the show was carried anywhere on broadcast yet, but I was hopeful.[46]

I knew I needed to reach out to the established activist world for a wider range of information sources – but who to interview? And how to get to them? I'd not been involved in the anti-nuclear movement before Fukushima, so I had no pre-existing connections. Cold calling the established names in the movement intimidated me – no fault of theirs, just my personal issues coming up – and I avoided contact with them for fear of sounding like a fool. As for the more accessible activists, I would contact them, fingers crossed that they'd get back to me. Sometimes yes, sometimes no. I was stymied as to how to proceed.

And then, a mistake on Facebook gave me my answer.

CHAPTER 12

GROWING THE SHOW

In August of 2011, just two months after starting *Nuclear Hotseat*, I read a brief post on Facebook about national nuclear activists holding a big fundraising concert in San Francisco, to be followed by a strategy meeting for California activists the next day. When I responded to it, Michael Mariotte, then head of Nuclear Information and Resource Service (NIRS), told me that the post was a mistake; the information was supposed to be private and sent only to movement groups and known activists. But after I explained my background and intent, he relented and gave me the when and where of it.

With no real credentials other than a not-yet-known podcast and Three Mile Island, I quickly arranged dog care, threw my sleeping bag in the car, and drove 400 miles up the coast. Arriving late at night, short on money and knowing no one to call, I slept in my car and the following morning cleaned up at a McDonalds.

Monday, August 8, 2011, I arrived at a library auditorium for the day's events. Instead of my usual brash self, I felt shy, not unlike a preteen at her first dance at a new school. Quietly taking a seat, I found myself next to a familiar face. I'd just seen a viral YouTube video featuring Kevin Kamps, the Nuclear Waste Watchdog of Beyond Nuclear, being interviewed about Fukushima by Thom Hartmann for RT.com. Summoning my courage, I introduced myself and said I wanted to interview him for a podcast he'd never heard of. The soul of kindness and gentility, he handed me his card, said he'd welcome my call, and would be happy to be interviewed.

Score! And the day's program hadn't even begun.

As we introduced ourselves around the room (65 anti-nuclear activists in one place!), I took notes on who sounded like they might make a good interview. I mentally raced to catch up with the alphabet soup they casually tossed around: BWR, PSR, IAEA, SONGS, NIRS.[47] Speakers went into depth on aspects of issues I'd heard mentioned at the Alliance for Survival evening: the dangers of embrittlement of reactor containment vessels from constant bombardment by radionuclides; regular "permitted" radioactive tritium leaks into groundwater around all reactors; uranium mining contamination on Native lands; harassment of nuclear industry whistleblowers who stand up for safety; and much more.[48]

On breaks, I'd rush up to people I'd identified based on their comments, push my iPod/stereo mic duo in front of their faces, and ask them for a brief message about nuclear "for my listeners" – all one of them – along with their name, the name of their organization, and contact information. Everyone seemed eager to talk with me, wanting to know more about the show and where they could find it.

I had carried with me the irrational fear that these seasoned activists would look at me as some interloper, a stranger not to be trusted, even rejected on suspicion of spying for pro-nuclear forces. It took me a while to relax into the fact that they actually welcomed me. As I came to realize, no one would *want* to be there if not compelled by some deeply personal anti-nuclear need.

Or perhaps they simply recognized in me another aging hippie who still wanted to change the world.

I drove back to Los Angeles that night with more than a dozen recordings to use in my next shows, along with commitments from numerous activists to be interviewed at length for future episodes of *Nuclear Hotseat*. More importantly, for the first time, I felt myself connected to a real-world activist community. I was no longer alone with the nuclear nightmare I'd been living for more than three decades. With these activists, I felt that I had found my home, my tribe.

As I continued producing *Nuclear Hotseat* on a weekly basis, I ramped up my involvement with the anti-nuclear community. I contacted the people I'd met in San Francisco, interviewed them, then asked for their suggestions of who else I might speak with for the show. They sent me on an anti-nuclear game of connect the dots. In the first year alone, I interviewed nuclear engineers, doctors, epidemiologists, a macrobiotic food distributor trying to guarantee the safety of imports from Japan, a California organic winemaker, whistleblowers, filmmakers, authors, politicians, and front line activists from all over the U.S. and around the world.

I expanded my Facebook connections by joining any group with "nuclear," "radiation," or "Fukushima" in its title and friending individuals whose posts I found intelligent, informed, compelling, and/or funny. My Facebook page started looking like a wire service – nuclear news with international reach. The first time I saw a post on my page in Japanese, I burst into tears. Someone in the country of Fukushima knew me, or at least knew the show.

For interviews, I'd track down, email, message, or call authors of articles or the people they cited. I introduced myself as Producer and Host of *Nuclear Hotseat,* sent them to the website, cited any creds I could muster. I rarely used the term "podcast" in describing the show, as at the time, that form of information dissemination was still considered by many to be disreputable.[49] I always bullet pointed a list of questions and asked if they wanted to add any specific questions for me to ask them. Some of the best information came from my spontaneous insights or glaring gaffes, which the speaker would then correct.

In essence, I was educating myself one interview at a time. I'd done the same thing at Broadway on Sunset, asking naïve questions until I could ask more intelligent ones. By doing it in front of an audio audience, I served as a kind of surrogate for whoever also wanted to learn. And producing the show felt oddly familiar until I realized that this was like doing *Closet Space,* only with digital instead of analogue technology.

Déjà vu all over again.

Slowly, organically, a format evolved.

I couldn't afford a license to use commercial music, so I started each show as a typical podcaster would: by simply talking. In the fall of 2011, in an article about San Onofre, I caught a reference to the warning sirens going off around that facility. Warning sirens?!? I immediately called the San

Onofre press office. Without going into details of who I was, I asked if there was a recording I could access. Within minutes, they sent me the link. I began using it to open the show that day. For the next two years, every *Nuclear Hotseat* started with that obnoxious siren going off, along with my ominous voiceover:

"That is the sound you never want to hear. It is the sound of the warning sirens going off at a nuclear reactor. When you hear that sound, suddenly you know that you are in the *Nuclear Hotseat*."

Interestingly, when I visited San Onofre with other activists for a Fukushima commemoration in March of 2012, I discovered that the each of the critical warning sirens for SanO's nuclear reactors was powered by an attached solar panel.

Think about it.[50]

For hard news, I scoured activist sites for links to articles, blog posts, videos, anything I could find that connected me with verifiable information from sources I could trust. I tried my best to sidestep echo-chamber exaggerations and conspiracy theory hysteria, and stick with the provable facts. Things at Fukushima and in the rest of the nuclear world were bad enough; no need for me to gild that radioactive lily.

As a fairly typical American, I'd rarely paid attention to news from other countries, and when some international story became newsworthy, I had no context beyond what was reported. But as I roamed the Internet, I accessed nuclear news from around the world: institutional cover-ups of radiation sickness in Japan in the wake of Fukushima; massive citizen pushback against new reactors at Koodankulam in India; Germany's leadership mandating immediate transition from nuclear to renewables; ongoing radiation devastation to the people of the Marshall Islands, where we nuked their homelands and instead of providing medical treatment to the displaced, irradiated natives, simply measured and studied the impact of radiation on their bodies – very Mengele.[51]

I became familiar with the foreign press: Britain's *The Guardian*, *Japan Times*, *Asahi Shinbun*, Australia's *Daily Telegraph*, *Times of India*, *Ottawa Citizen*, and more. I developed a fondness for the London-based Reuters news agency, always notable for the clarity, intelligence, and consistency of their nuclear coverage. Associated Press reports on Fukushima started strong and the news service generated lots of investigative pieces on the U.S. nuclear industry. But this early enthusiasm for the topic rapidly faded to where AP rarely shows up on my radar for any nuclear story, and hasn't for several years.

Seen through a nuclear lens, this exposure to other perspectives permanently shifted my understanding of how the world works. It was not a pleasant awakening.

After building a pull file of the week's news stories, on Tuesday – production day – I'd print out everything, combine sources, edit, and compile the newscast. Japan, U.S., and International news fell into neat categories, and I quickly realized that many of the issues faced in one location were consistently faced by people close to nuclear facilities around the world.

Some of the nuclear stories I read on air were so blatantly unbelievable – yet true! – that I reached for a word I'd never before in my life used: Numnutz. I started incorporating it into my comments on the most egregious of each week's news stories. That turned into a weekly mini-rant, complete with moans, groans, sound effects and, when appropriate, Yiddish.

One week, as I finished reading yet another story of nuclear absurdity, I thumped a rhythm on my desk, chanted, "Num-nutz-of-the-Week!" and said, "I'm going to have to record that some day." By the fall of 2013, I had done just that: written and recorded both the Numnutz jingle and the *Nuclear Hotseat* theme song. They've been in weekly use ever since. [52]

I guess my musical theatre years weren't entirely wasted.

Other features evolved. Among the activists I met on Facebook was Erica Gray of the Nuclear Free Campaign of the Sierra Club. Erica follows the NRC Event Notification Reports, a daily compilation of incidents and accidents at reactors that the operators must, by law, report.[53] She posts the notifications pertinent to reactor issues on social media. Not a week goes by without things going wrong, sometimes terribly wrong, at nuclear reactors around the country.[54]

In one instance, at the Pilgrim nuclear power facility at the foot of Cape Cod in Massachusetts, there had been an incursion into adjacent waters by an unknown, un-permitted vessel. The NRC labeled it "A Potential Security Event." Security and police turned out in force and intercepted a small boat with some duck hunters who had accidentally wandered too close to the reactor.[55]

I read the story and then, to enhance the seriousness of this emergency response, announced that *Nuclear Hotseat* had tracked down an eyewitness to the incident and secured an exclusive interview.

I then played a series of duck calls.[56]

Buh-dum-bump – CHING!

This led to me periodically compiling reactor stories into the DUCK!-and-Cover Report, named in an homage to the rightfully-lambasted 1951 Bert the Turtle Civil Defense film.[57] It instructed school children to protect themselves in case of a nuclear explosion by simply ducking under their desks and covering their heads with their hands.[58] Right – like that's going to do any good in the middle of a thermonuclear fireball that would collapse, if not evaporate, school buildings and everything else. (Animation genius Brad Bird wickedly parodied Duck and Cover in his 1999 masterpiece, *The Iron Giant*.)

The DUCK!-and-Cover report summarizes recent NRC event reports on whatever has gone wrong THIS week at our aging, decrepit fleet of power reactors. Remember, this atrociously expensive technology splits the atom to generate heat to boil water to make steam to power generators to make electricity that goes to the house that Jack built. These "teapots"[59] were designed and built to operate for only 40 years before decommissioning. This time limit was common knowledge. Engineers warned that after four decades, the reactors would no longer be safe to run because of "nuclear engine fatigue" – embrittlement of the steel containment structure that could cause it to crack. Even microscopic cracking of containment would lead to deadly radiation releases, if not more severe accidents.

Think of it this way: In light of engine fatigue, would you trust a 40-year old car on a high speed, cross-country highway trip?

But the nuclear industry wants its cash cows to continue operating and making the moolah, estimated as a profit of $1-million a day *per reactor*. With that much money at stake, it's no surprise that reactor operators have applied for 20-year license extensions rather than pay attention to the original engineers' safety warnings. And the NRC, that poster child for regulatory capture,[60] has fallen into lock step with nuclear industry demands. To date, the NRC has approved 74 of those 20-year license extensions to our 99 currently operating reactors. NRC has never turned down a single application for license extension. Presumably, the operators of the other 25 reactors just haven't asked for their extensions. Yet.

The Pilgrim Nuclear Power Station in Plymouth, Massachusetts, is the exact same GE Mark I reactor as the ones that melted down at Fukushima. The facility is officially ranked by the Nuclear Regulatory Commission as THE WORST RUN nuclear reactor in the country and has held this dubious honor since 2015.[61] Pilgrim sits at the foot of Cape Cod, and should there be an accident and radiation release, evacuation would be virtually impossible, as anyone who's been stuck in weekend traffic getting off the Cape could attest. Pilgrim is licensed to run through 2019, even though a private email from the NRC's lead inspector[62] that was accidentally distributed to Diane Turco,[63] co-founder of the activist group Cape Downwinders, lamented: "Many staff across the site may not have the standards to know what 'good' actually is… The plant seems overwhelmed just trying to run the station." Turco immediately forwarded the email to Christine Legere, ace reporter on Pilgrim for the *Cape Cod Times*, and the story resulted in headlines around the world… but no change in policy or timeline for Pilgrim.

Then there's Indian Point, with two nuclear reactors only 35 miles from Manhattan. It's generally conceded that

YES, I GLOW IN THE DARK

Indian Point's reactors and spent fuel pools were the second choice of target for the second plane on 9/11. But a terrorist attack isn't the only problem the facility faces. Indian Point been running under expired licenses since September, 2013 (Unit 2), and December, 2015 (Unit 3). The operators have stopped pushing for 20-year extensions because Indian Point is supposed to shut down as of 2021, so hey, it might just as well run on an expired license. Oh, and now there's a gas pipeline running next to the nuclear reactors and its two open, vulnerable spent fuel pools and dry cask storage canisters – each of which holds roughly a Chernobyl-worth of radioactive cesium 137 in every can.[64] Hey, Indian Point's only going to be operating for a few more years; what could go wrong?[65]

NOTE: That is a question you *never* want to ask around nukes.

But wait! There's more! Not satisfied that they've gotten approval to run these rustbucket reactors for 20 years past their use-by date, the nuclear industry has been laying tracks for an *additional* 20-year extension per reactor – meaning a total operating span of 80 YEARS! Sometimes they've had the gall to push this agenda under the rubric: "Is there life after 60?"

Yuk yuk.

Now let me ask you: if you wouldn't trust a 40-60-let-alone-80-year-old car to operate safely and reliably at high speed on today's highways, how in the world could anyone trust the safety of these antique nuclear reactors? If anything went wrong with a car, it would simply break down or crash, hopefully harming few people, if any. But if a nuclear reactor containment suffers even a microscopic crack, it will release massive amounts of deadly radiation, in which case the damage is going to be a whole lot worse than a car crash... and the consequences will last forever.[66]

The 40-year operating limit has been a well-known and documented engineering limitation since the 1950's, when "Atoms for Peace" nuclear reactors were first envisioned and construction begun.[67]

But to cover their tracks and spin-speak the public – including reporters who don't know enough to know that they don't know enough – the NRC has re-written its own history. It now claims on its website (emphasis added): "This original 40-year term for reactor licenses *was based on economic and antitrust considerations not on limitations of nuclear technology.*"[68] Absolutely not true! It was the limits of safe operation of the nuclear technology that caused the restriction on allowable years of operation. But there's the agency's blatant revisionism in plain sight, right there in black-and-white pixels, in full service to their nuclear industry masters.

Like that Disney demonstration with ping pong balls, every story I reported led to at least two others, with no end in sight. As I roamed the nuclear landscape, I managed to snag an amazing array of interviews for the show. Among them:

- I interviewed Dr. Caldicott a number of times and eventually was able to do so without stammering.
- I got the truth about how the World Health Organization (WHO) minimized the impact of Chernobyl from Alison Katz of Geneva, Switzerland-based Independent WHO, and a counter to WHO's minimizing of Fukushima from Berlin-based Dr. Alex Katz of International Physicians for the Prevention of Nuclear War.

- Prof. Robert "Bo" Jacobs of the Hiroshima Peace Institute spoke movingly about the problems faced by *hibakusha*, the survivors of the Hiroshima and Nagasaki A-bombs.
- Produced anniversary specials on Three Mile Island, Chernobyl, and Fukushima. The annual Fukushima commemoration is Voices from Japan, an elaborate production produced and coordinated with Beverly Findlay-Kanko of Families for Safe Energy. New every year, it consists of a full-length program of interviews in Japanese on specific issues not being covered even in alternative media. They are then translated into English, after which a crew of Japanese-born professional voiceover actors read their words. These Japanese/English audios are combined with a context-creating script and present an honest view of what is currently going on with Fukushima evacuees and victims in Japan.
- Did specials on news stories as they broke, including hurricanes and torrential rains at Texas nuclear facilities, radiation spills at the Hanford Site in Washington state, the 55 gallon drum of radioactive waste that exploded and contaminated the Waste Isolation Pilot Plant near Carlsbad, New Mexico, ongoing nuclear incompetence at the Pilgrim site in Massachusetts, and more.
- I traveled to cover stories: Dr. Caldicott's two New York Academy of Science symposia; the North St. Louis struggles by activist mothers of the Just Moms group against radioactive contamination of Coldwater Creek and illegally buried high level radioactive WWII nuclear weapons waste at their neighborhood West Lake Landfill.

- I attended the University of Chicago's orgy of self-congratulations over the 75th anniversary of the building of the first atomic pile, commemorated with a fireworks display that mimicked the bomb that was exploded over the site – a gesture both wrongheaded and tone deaf.
- MC'ed a rally in D.C. on the National Mall before walking over to lobby members of Congress.
- And for a bit of fun along with the work, flew to Canada where I met activists gathered from around the world in Quebec City for the combined World Uranium Symposium and International Uranium Film Festival.

Among just a few of the more memorable interviews: Naoto Kan, former Prime Minister of Japan during Fukushima; Mitsuhei Murata, former Japanese ambassador to Switzerland; Alexey Yablakov, the "Grandfather of Russian Environmentalism" and the man responsible for the western world knowing what really happened as a result of Chernobyl; Rachel Bronson, head of the Bulletin of the Atomic Scientists on the story behind the Doomsday Clock, which measures how close humanity is to self-annihilation; anything with Arnie Gundersen, former nuclear industry insider and Chief Engineer at Fairewinds Energy Education; and too many more to count.

Pretty staggering stuff for me and My Little Podcast. Such good people, fighting so hard and so long against nuclear… and still, the industry prospered, no matter how awful their transgressions against people and the environment, literally around the world. As I learned more and more, I could not help but wonder:

What else does the nuclear industry get away with? And how do they keep getting away with it?

CHAPTER 13

WHAT THE NUCLEAR INDUSTRY GETS AWAY WITH

The interlinking issues of nuclear began coalescing for me into a godawful picture of what it does. Because radiation is invisible and takes years if not decades for its damage to appear, it's easy for so-called "experts" to hide, ignore, or denigrate its devastation to health. Cause separated from effect by a long enough time makes it easy to not recognize radiation as the source of health problems, and hard to prove the connection if you do.

That doesn't mean it's not happening. As we've been involved with nuclear matters for more than 70 years, the impact of early radiation contamination is only now making itself known. What I discovered was a not a pretty picture.

To cite just a few of my early revelations:

- Uranium mining left vast amounts of radioactive waste unremediated and open to the elements, where it sank into the groundwater or blew around as dust. The local populations that mined it, usually indigenous tribal people (Native Americans in the U.S., First Nations members in Canada, aboriginal people in Australia) developed cancer, heart disease, auto-immune problems, birth defects, fertility problems, and more at an alarming rate. All these health conditions are known to be caused by exposure to radiation. As is said by Native American activists such as Leona Morgan of the Diné (Navaho) people, "You may meet old coal miners, but you will never meet an old uranium miner."

- Radiation releases from nuclear reactors into the environment are legally "permitted" by the NRC, though nobody asked permission of you or me, and I certainly would not grant it. Reactor operators are allowed to release radioactive tritium into groundwater and radon into the air without any notice to the surrounding community. Epidemiological studies routinely reveal elevated cancer risks to those who lived, worked, or grew up in proximity to any nuclear reactor.[69]

- Radiation release levels spike during reactor refueling – when so-called "spent" fuel rods are removed to pools of cooling water and new ones installed. That's when nuclear reactors emit the highest level of radionuclides that contaminate the surrounding communities and create the greatest risk. But no notice is ever given to a community as to exactly when refueling will take place, so local citizens are unable to take specific protective actions. Worse, the NRC averages out each reactor's radiation release levels over a full year, thus creating reports that mask the concentrated short-term dose from refueling in a much-diluted annual average. This makes radiation exposure levels in communities around a nuclear reactor seem negligible and harmless when, during refueling, they most definitely are not.

- The elephant in the nuclear industry's livingroom is the dangerous radioactive waste it creates. There is no known way to safely contain and/or store the highly radioactive, plutonium-containing "spent" reactor fuel rods until they are no longer radioactive. That's because plutonium has a half-life of 24,000 years and requires ten to twenty half-life cycles before it becomes harmless – meaning 240,000 to 480,000 years.[70] By comparison, the whole of human recorded history spans, at most, 5,000 years. So those "spent" fuel rods still have a lot of radioactivity to "spend."

- Why is plutonium so dangerous? To cite award-winning journalist Karl Grossman's superb book, *COVER UP: What you ARE NOT SUPPOSED to KNOW ABOUT NUCLEAR POWER,*[71] in a section he sourced from Dr. Helen Caldicott's research: "A pound of plutonium, released as airborne dust, has the potential to cause fatal lung cancer in nine billion people. An ounce (only a tablespoonful, because plutonium is very heavy) can kill 200 million people. A millionth of a gram of plutonium will cause cancer." So how much plutonium comes from your average nuclear reactor? While specifics vary based on size of reactor and years of operation, on average, each nuclear power plant produces *between 400 to 500 pounds of Plutonium-239 a year.* At any one time during its operation, depending upon the age of the core, up to 1,000 pounds of Plutonium 239 can be on site, and tons of radioactive material sit in the so-called "spent" fuel pool.[72] That's a lot of tablespoons. So every nuclear reactor's on-site waste can accurately be considered a repository for a potential planetary dose of lethal radiation.

- Another characteristic of radioactive material is what's sometimes called the "Nuclear Midas Touch."[73] In the Greek myth, everything King Midas touched turned to gold. Inevitably, he starved to death because, let's face it, despite the culinary pretentions of super chef Gordon Ramsey and his ilk, you can't eat gold. In the same way, everything a radioactive substance touches inevitably becomes radioactive itself. If radwaste is held away from the environment in a container, that container eventually becomes radioactive and has to be encased in another container, which eventually becomes radioactive and has to be encased in another container... etc. That's why the Chernobyl disaster site required a second containment structure after the first emergency sarcophagus, predicted to last only 30 years, started decaying right on schedule. This new one, optimistically called the New Safe Confinement, cost $1.6 billion and will only be good for about 100 years. Then it, too will need another, larger containment structure, turning the disaster site into the nuclear version of Russian nesting *matryoshka* dolls.[74]

- As for neutralizing radioactive elements already in the nuclear industry's waste stream, there is currently no known way to do it. More shockingly, there is no known government or private enterprise program promoting research into radiation neutralization. As a result, charlatans and scammers have found it open season to claim to have invented their own "top secret process capable of neutralizing Fukushima's radiation!" – all without providing any science, scalable models, or data. They never expose their information to or talk with activists or anyone with the genuine knowledge to see through their mumbo-jumbo. What they do provide are unending requests for money, which the gullible – especially, as I've found, in the entertainment industry – have been known to provide.[75]

- There's a big difference between the health impact of internal and external radiation exposure. The nuclear industry relies on external exposure models for its assurances of "no danger," but this doesn't address the problem of ionizing radiation from nuclear facilities, uranium mining, or any other source getting into our food and/or water and, from there, inside our bodies. In the ocean, radiation gets taken up by plankton and seaweed, which are eaten by small fish, which are eaten by larger fish, on up the food chain into the species we humans eat, with the radiation dose bioaccumulating every step of the way. Result: Internal contamination, where the released stream of radioactive particles machineguns the adjacent cells and organs, creating damage down to our DNA.

- Same problem when radioactive particles rain out over land. Once on the ground as rain or snow, water carries the radioactive atoms deep into the soil, where they can be taken up by plants, including agricultural crops, landing in our fruits and vegetables. These particles also contaminate feedstock that gets eaten by animals that are slaughtered for meat, or kept for their milk or eggs. By eating or drinking anything that results from this contaminated food chain, one is exposed to an internal dose of radiation. If even a single atom lodges anywhere in the body, there's no distance between hot sprays of subatomic particles and vital organs.

- All radiation exposure is cumulative. In addition to obvious sources of exposure from mining, manufacturing, bombs, reactors, and transport, this includes medical sources such as x-rays, PET scans, and CT scans. That means that though the nuclear industry and governments downplay radiation releases and contamination risks as "small," "insignificant," and "not a danger to human health," *every* exposure contributes to an ever-accumulating risk that can, indeed, prove "significant" to one's health.

- No insurance company will indemnify you from damages resulting from a nuclear anything. The insurance industry isn't dumb; they knew an unwinnable game when they saw one and opted out early. Check the nuclear clause in your homeowner's policy. Didn't know you had one? Think that's a mistake?

- And a reminder that 100 aboveground nuclear detonations were committed at the Nevada Test Site between 1951 and 1963. That means that, as a country, the United States nuked ourselves, with radiation releases that wafted over Nevada, into Utah, and from there onto parts east, north and south, as well as into the jet stream where it continues to plague us today.

There was much more. My denial system died hard, but week after week of revelations about nuclear interests playing loose-and-fast with our planetary future forced me to face these and many other difficult truths. And I wondered: The problems with every aspect of the nuclear industry were so blatant, so consistent, so dangerous – how did they get away with it? And why does the public not know about what's happening?

The answer – beyond money, lobbyists, money, campaign contributions, money, on-demand PR hacks, money, blatant lies, and, oh yes, money – is best conveyed by quoting Shakespeare's *Hamlet*:

"Words, words, words."

CHAPTER 14

HOW THE INDUSTRY GETS AWAY WITH IT: NUCLEAR SPIN-SPEAK

The nuclear industry plays a linguistic shill game to hide their ugly truths in plain sight. They use neuro-linguistic programming (NLP) and languaging tricks to keep us from noticing how nakedly radioactive that nuclear man behind the curtain really is. Some of this wording sleight-of-hand is found in virtually every pronouncement by the nuclear industry, picked up and used intact by an uncritical media.

I call it Nuclear Spin-Speak, deliberate wording choices intended to make us so confused that we don't or can't discern difficult nuclear truths.

Among the industry's top linguistic tricks to gaslight us:

- "Significant" – Any time a problem is reported, the word "*significant*" is inserted with a negative in front of it, as in, "No *significant* radiation leak" or "Not a *significant* danger." But that's not the same as *no* radiation leak or *no* danger. According to the National Academy of Science's gold standard report,

BEIR VII: Health Risks from Exposure to Low Levels of Ionizing Radiation,[76] there is *no* level of radiation below which exposure is safe. Because the damaging health effects of radiation are lifelong and cumulative, there is no such thing as a *NOT* "*significant*" dose. "Negative + *significant*" is a word combo meant to deflect fear and discourage closer examination of what's being reported. Otherwise known as the gaslighting condescension of, "There there Missy, don't worry your pretty little head about it."

- "Immediate," as in, "No *immediate* danger to health or safety." Literally speaking, that is correct. Unless one is exposed to a catastrophic level of radiation, the effects take time to show up – years, even decades, or generations. So unless one is a first responder at a nuclear disaster, like Chernobyl liquidators or one of the Fukushima Fifty, radiation-induced health problems may not show up for years – not *immediately*, but they will show up over time. In our ADHD society, this deployment of "Negative + *immediate*" is usually enough to deflect criticism and prevent us from believing anything could be seriously wrong. But now, since *immediate* has become so well known as a suspect word, the industry has moved on in the thesaurus to *imminent*.[77] The rest of Roget is sure to follow.

- Minimizing adjectives. The nuclear industry loooooves 'em! Whenever a problem shows up at a reactor, they immediately lower our perception of its importance by the judicious application of such adjectives as "*small*," "*brief*," "*inconsequential*," or the current noun-of-choice to describe the amount plutonium that contaminated 42 workers in 2017 at the Hanford site in Washington State: *"specks."*[78] My local NPR station repeatedly referred to San Onofre's[79] radiation leak on January 31, 2012, as "tiny" – the exact word used in Southern California Edison's initial press releases.

- But because of radiation's cumulative effect on health, *no* leak of *any* size is acceptable at a nuclear reactor. Indeed, that "tiny" leak at SanO ultimately proved big enough to indicate design flaws in two new steam generators, which led to the permanent shut-down of both reactors.[80] [81] So any time you hear word of a nuclear accident or leak referred to as *"tiny," "small,"* or any of their minimizing kin, skip the adjective and stick with the noun: "leak" or "accident."

- "Nuclear Oversight" – I have to laugh at the straight-faced use of this word by the NRC and the nuclear industry, because *"oversight"* has two completely opposite meanings:
  - Over*seeing* – the action of supervising, watching over, directing, or supervising.
  - Over*looking* – a failure to notice or act.

This has got to be some wonk's idea of a joke, because whether one believes that the NRC is doing a good job (over*see*ing) or an incompetent job (over*look*ing), the word *"oversight"* is correct.

- *"Spent"* Fuel – When something is *"spent,"* it means it's gone, done, powerless, inert. *"Spent"* fuel makes it sound like the nuclear waste has exhausted its ability to do any damage, doesn't it? Yet all *"spent"* fuel is highly radioactive and contains, as a byproduct, Plutonium 239, which can be used to make a dirty bomb or refined into weapons-grade plutonium – and it takes only a small amount of Plutonium-239 to fuel a nuclear weapon.[82] That's a "significant" amount of radioactive material to "spend."

- Fuel rods must sit around immersed in water in a *"spent* fuel" pool for a minimum of five years before they're cool enough to be placed in dry casks for marginally safer storage. But what's called high-burn-up fuel – basically Super High Octane as opposed to Regular – takes at least two additional years to cool down enough. So while these rods are no longer useful as fuel for a nuclear reactor, each still has plenty of radioactive material left to *"spend."*

- *"Permitted* releases" – This term for regular, expected radiation releases from nuclear reactors carries two meanings: that the releases have been allowed (adjective), and that they have been given authorization to do this action (noun – as in "a *permit"*). It implies that all due diligence has been done and everyone is A-OK with whatever radiation release takes place. But nobody asked me if I gave permission for radiation to be released, let alone without notification or warning, and I'm willing to bet nobody asked you, either. See, we're not important enough to be consulted on corporate issues that directly impact our lives. Somebody, somewhere, must have given their permission, but nobody will cop to it and it's rarely questioned because, after all, these releases are *"permitted."*

- Slippery Slope Wording – One intentional misdirecting phrase used repeatedly in connection with Fukushima is "The worst nuclear disaster *since Chernobyl.*" The truth is that Fukushima is not only the worst nuclear disaster ever, it is the worst industrial accident ever – and it's far from over. Three nuclear reactors in meltdown (though we refer to the Fukushima nuclear accident in the singular as if only one reactor were involved). Radioactive water leaking into the ocean continuously since March 11, 2011. Radioactivity so high that the melted-down units can only be entered by robots, which usually fry before being able to send back any useful information. Fukushima is, at minimum, Chernobyl times three. But then, it's not coming from the then-feared and hated Russians but from our Japanese allies, as well as General Electric and Westinghouse, American companies involved in the design and build. So to the media and in the public's perception, Fukushima ranks as nuclear disaster #2.[83]
- Confusing Technical Terms – Depending on whether the nuclear industry is referring to emitted radiation, radiation dose, or biological risk of radiation exposure, a different term will be used: rads, rems, Bequerels, Sieverts, Curies, grays, and milli- and/or micro- quantities of each.[84] That makes it difficult for even knowledgeable people to compare resulting readings without goggling the terms and equivalencies. For the general public, the numbers blur by, without anyone understanding what exactly is being measured and what the results mean. Not a bad tactic if you want to confuse the public's ability

to understand how badly our health and genetic future may have been compromised.

Then there are the words that have been purged from nuclear discourse:

- *"Atomic"* – When focus groups discovered that the word *"atomic"* had too many negative associations – as in The Bomb – the entire industry changed its names. Almost every mention of *"atomic"* morphed to "nuclear."[85] And POOF! A generation of *"atomic"*-based fears were semantically whitewashed out of our remembered history and consciousness. Just. Like. That.
- *"Fallout"* – The word *"fallout"* was one of the first words to be unofficially but widely banned from news reports after Fukushima. One outraged reporter for a major market TV station was told directly by his news director to expunge the word from his coverage of the radiation plume coming over the Pacific from Japan… and while he was at it, not to use the word *"plume"* either. The only time *"fallout"* could be used was in relation to a politician's bad behavior, as in "the fallout from former Rep. Anthony Weiner's wiener pics."
- *"Partial* Meltdown" – At Three Mile Island, the accident was dubbed a *"partial"* meltdown, which is like saying a woman is a little bit pregnant. No such thing exists. You're either pregnant or you're not, and there was either a meltdown or there wasn't – and there *was* a meltdown at TMI. It just didn't extend to *all* of the fuel rods. Yet by surgically

attaching the word *"partial,"* the nuclear perpetrators have made it appear that TMI was a "less-than" accident, not serious, not *"significant."*

The Nuclear Regulatory Commission has its own word soup of spin-speak. Some recent examples:

- "Waste *Confidence* Hearings" – When the NRC started holding public hearings on what to do about the used radioactive fuel rods, one would expect the title of such gatherings to be something like the simple "Waste Hearings." But that's not manipulative enough, so the NRC inserted the word *"confidence"* in the middle of their keyword phrase. Why? Semantically speaking, might it be to set up a subliminal mandate to consider this a *confidence*-building process, implying that we had *"confidence"* in the NRC and their handling of waste? Activists refer to these meetings as "Waste *Con-job* Hearings" or "Waste *No-Confidence* Hearings." The last thing that any informed individual has about the NRC's handling of nuclear waste is *"confidence."*
- Similarly, the ongoing hearings regarding the con game being played on ratepayers in southern California regarding San Onofre go under the title "Community Engagement Meetings." Activists refer to these as "Community *Enragement* Meetings," for the blatant manipulation intended to negate the public's voice, including: hiring the slowest, most boring moderator they could to disengage attention; scheduling community feedback for after the break, when virtually all media had disappeared and so major points of contention were not reported upon;

and the ongoing, condescending "There there, Missy, we know what we're talking about and you don't" attitude taken by NRC officials, who have been described as "the gaslighting mansplainers at the podium."

Within the Nuclear Regulatory Commission, Nuclear Spin-Speak has long been institutionalized. Consider the wording developed to refer to accidents at reactors, a four-level Emergency Classification scale, none of which sounds particularly alarming:

- Level 1: "Notification of Unusual Event" – A brief review of the NRC's accident logs clearly demonstrates that there is nothing more usual than an "*Unusual*" Event at a U.S. nuclear reactor; at least one happens just about every week. I'm convinced the NRC uses this palliative, diminishing word to make it seem like it's a rarity, nothing important has happened, "stop being so emotional and don't worry your pretty little head about that problem at your local N-plant."
- Level 2: "Alert" – This word choice implies, "Okay, we already told you a problem like this is '*unusual*,' but we're putting some additional attention on it, so no need for you to put any attention here." Since Level 2 is halfway up the NRC's designation ladder, one would think the agency and facility operators should be more on the offensive rather than simply "*alert*."
- Level 3: "Site Area Emergency" – Makes it sound like there's just a little problem confined to the facility,

doesn't it? But in the wording of the NRC, it means: "actual or likely major failures of plant functions needed for protection of the public... that could lead to the likely failure of or that prevent effective access to, equipment needed for the protection of the public."[86] Meaning that the problem is so bad, they can't guarantee the public's safety. That's you and me.

But even more outrageously, the NRC adds, "Any releases [of radiation] are not expected to result in exposure levels which exceed EPA PAG exposure levels *beyond the site boundary*."[87] Right, like radiation knows where the boundary of the reactor facility is and will *stop right there*! Just as realistic as those olde cartoons showing a car driving through rain and snow until it crosses the border into California, and then it immediately becomes a sunny, dry, beautiful day.

- Level 4: "General Emergency" – The Big Kahuna, a Three Mile Island equivalent, or worse. Somehow, the term doesn't quite match up with the NRC's own description of a General Emergency's reality: "Events are in progress or have occurred which involve *actual or imminent substantial core degradation* or *melting with potential for loss of containment integrity* or hostile action that results in an *actual loss of physical control of the facility*."[88] In other words, head for the hills! The Nuke's busted!

On *Nuclear Hotseat*, every time I announce an Unusual Event, I always add the line, "Nothing is more usual than an NRC Unusual Event at a nuclear reactor." I then take the opportunity to talk about these classifications towards potential apocalypse, always referring to the Level 4 "General Emergency" as "Kiss Your Ass Goodbye."

These industry wording tricks play into the projection of nuclear power as being (what they would like us to believe) a "clean!" "green!" "sustainable!" "safe!" energy source – when the truth is quite the opposite. (More on that in a moment.)

Why would the NRC, a government agency which is tasked with protecting "people and the environment," automatically kowtow to nuclear industry licensing desires, semantically help them cover their tracks, and rubberstamp every request they make, no matter how ill-conceived? Could it perhaps be because *the NRC receives 90% of its funding from the nuclear industry?*[89]

Yes, you read that right. The money is collected from nuclear reactor owners and operators "for specific NRC services, such as licensing and inspection, (and…) an annual fee for generic regulatory expenses and other costs not recovered through fees for specific services."[90] The more nuclear reactors are operating and the longer they operate, the more money comes into the NRC, guaranteeing its survival as an agency. So in order for the hens to maintain their henhouse – meaning NRC employees not lose their jobs to closed reactors and no new builds – they follow the specifications ordered up by the nuclear fox.[91]

Additionally, NRC Commissioners are generally hard core members of the nuclear industry. After serving their one or two five-year terms as regulators, they usually return to the industry to reap their rewards. Traditionally, these post-NRC jobs come with an enormous bump in salary and perks for industry-compliant commissioners – plenty of motivation not to screw up their golden parachute by doing something as silly as standing up for long-term safety, let alone common sense, at nuclear reactors. Anyone who doesn't play by those rules find the nuclear employment revolving door slammed in their face, as former NRC Chair Gregory Jaczko found out the hard way.[92]

Of course, the biggest nuclear industry con job is to have co-opted the words "clean!" "green!" "sustainable!" – and somehow "a solution to global warming!"

HOGWASH! Let's take this one apart:

Clean? How can anything be clean when it generates DNA-destroying, cancer-causing radioactive waste that will take 24,000 years to decay to a level even HALF as deadly as it is to begin with? But the nuclear industry cunningly controls the languaging and points of reference, narrowly defining "clean" to mean, "carbon-free in the generation of the electricity." It ignores and covers up carbon emissions from the nuclear fuel cycle, including uranium mining, transport, refining, manufacturing, transport between sites (they ain't using electric vehicles, I can assure you), construction of nuclear reactors, and daily operations.

What – you didn't know that nuclear reactors don't generate their own electricity but have to pull it from the grid, just like the rest of us? That's what took Fukushima down: loss of offsite power and then the flooding which destroyed the emergency diesel generators. That's what allowed the three reactors to overheat and melt down.

This "carbon-free" lie also doesn't take into account the carbon toll created during decommissioning and the never-ending need for storage of radioactive waste. When you think about it, does this strike you as "clean!" or "green!"? I sure don't think so. Oh, but it is "sustainable," in that the radioactive waste will sustain itself in its threat to life and health virtually FOREVER.

But of course, those legislators who take the nuclear perpetrators' words (and perhaps other incentives) at face value are more than happy to fork over taxpayer dollars meant to be invested in genuinely clean, green, sustainable energy forces (e.g. solar, wind, hydro-electric, geothermal, tidal, etc.). All this to keep aging, embrittled nuclear reactors online beyond their design limitations and safety margins... and money flowing into the pockets of owners and shareholders.

As for nuclear being some kind of get-out-of-jail-free card for global warming, that's ludicrous. Arnie Gundersen, Chief Engineer of Fairewinds Energy Education and a former industry insider, explains that with the time it takes to build a nuclear reactor – even if everything is achieved on budget and on schedule, which it never is – given the speed at which global warming is accelerating, there is no way nuclear technology could ever be able to make any kind of difference. And of course, even those highly industry-flogged New! Cute! Small Modular Reactors (sounds like Lego units, doesn't it?) represent a totally untried technology, never built, unproven, that would, of course, come with the usual, eternal attendant radioactive waste problems.[93] (*Nuclear Hotseat* carried Arnie's comprehensive analysis of the "nuclear cure for global warming" lie on episode #338 from December 12, 2017 – and Arnie was stunning in both his clarity and brevity.[94])

But of all the nuclear propaganda to manipulate public perception, none was as prescient – or, in my estimation, evil – as that which was instituted at the very start of the nuclear age. When the Trinity test – the first nuclear detonation – was held near Alamogordo, New Mexico on July 16, 1945, something had to be done to explain the sudden enormous explosion in the middle of the desert. William Lawrence, science reporter for the *New York Times*, was brought in by the government to write a cover-up press release.[95]

Lawrence invented a fiction that blamed the early morning blast on an ammunition dump accident. It worked to explain away the incident and diffuse interest, with no one questioning how a munitions dump explosion could be seen over 1,000 miles away.

Then "Atomic Bill" Lawrence was put on the U.S. government payroll at the *exact same time* he was being paid by the *New York Times* (a clear conflict of journalist ethics). His assignment: to write a series of ten press releases on the wonders of this new Atomic Age, how the bomb had been miraculously built, and why we needed it. The series was held until after both the Hiroshima and Nagasaki bombs were dropped, and included Lawrence's eyewitness account of the bombing of Nagasaki from one of the follow planes.

With only minimal editing, these unfailingly laudatory articles ran in the *New York Times* with no mention of their government PR/propaganda connection. Then the *Times*, in cooperation with the government, distributed these articles FOR FREE to any publication that wanted them. Coming as they did under the byline the *New York Times'* respected science writer, they were accepted and reprinted unquestioningly. Nobody knew to notice that these "articles" said *not one word* about the deadly post-detonation impact of radiation on the survivors of Hiroshima and Nagasaki. Lawrence hewed to the government line and avoided the subject of radioactivity almost entirely, except for a few inconsequential, passing mentions, instead couching his descriptions of atomic bombs in nationalistic boosterism laced with ecstatic biblical references.

These free articles were uncritically published virtually everywhere and became our country's baseline for understanding all things nuclear – propaganda that skewed policy from the very start. It even won Lawrence a Pulitzer Prize.[96] Within a year, atmospheric testing of nuclear weapons began to country-wide approval. Meanwhile, Manhattan Project scientists feeling guilty for the hell-on-earth they had unleashed explored "peaceful" uses for their deadly technology and landed on using the heat of nuclear reactions to boil water to turn steam generators to create electricity. It also had the benefit of shunting the government's expense of creating weapons-grade plutonium onto an unsuspecting, well-propagandized public.

The only honest newspaper report on the aftermath of the atomic bombs dropped on Japan came from Australian journalist Wilfred Burchett. He inadvertently became the first western journalist to enter Hiroshima, three weeks after the bomb was dropped. It was a fluke that he avoided the tightening U.S. military protocols – meaning censorship – that controlled reporters' access and mobility. Burchett's resulting story was headlined in four inch type across the front page of the London *Daily Express*: "THE ATOMIC PLAGUE: 'I Write This As a Warning to the World.'

DOCTORS FALL AS THEY WORK" and a picture of the bombing devastation captioned, "This Picture Does Not Tell the Whole Story."[97]

Burchett could not have made the truth of the atomic bomb and the "plague" of radiation poisoning any more plain. But long before Twitter and instantaneous real-time global communications, his words were isolated to one newspaper in London. And let's face it, especially in 1945, who are you going to listen to – some Aussie journalist who works for a single newspaper[98] or the *New! York! Times! Science! Reporter!?*

So by using the manufactured, propagandized echo chamber of those government and media manipulated stories, our unquestioning acceptance of all things nuclear was hard-wired into American hearts and minds, even before The Bombs were dropped on Japan. And after we incinerated and irradiated hundreds of thousands of people in Japan, never was heard a discouraging word… unless you happened to catch Burchett's story.

The fix was in from the start.

Keep these manipulations of perception in mind whenever you watch, listen to, or read news dealing with nuclear issues. This is especially true if the interview you're hearing is with so-called "experts" drawn from the nuclear industry and its allies.

Indeed, the final Nuclear Spin-Speak word is *"activist,"* as though it's somehow suspect that a regular citizen would take the time, energy, and personal resources to become educated and conversant in a complex, arcane technology in order to engage in conversation, debate and protest. But that's when you need to ask yourself: who do you find more credible? Someone representing a multibillion dollar industry whose hefty salary depends on its continuance who tells you there's nothing to worry about? Or citizens, neighbors, mothers, fathers, grandparents who are so moved by concern and alarm at what they're being subjected to that they research, study, learn, and share what they can, giving with all their heart and soul without any hope of compensation, in the hope of stopping something horrible from happening... or if it's already happened, getting worse?

The lesson being:

- If you encounter a report on nuclear issues that uses any of these spin-speak words or phrases, it's always safest to suspect that the situation is much worse than what's being reported. Actually, IMHO, you can't go wrong taking that stance regarding any nuclear story.
- If you're reporting on a nuclear situation, edit out the abovementioned spin-speak language so you don't inadvertently play into the industry's PR game plan and pass along their manipulations of perception. Always remain skeptical of their assurances.
- Also if you're reporting, try starting your stories with the community/activist perspective and their experts before letting the industry try to justify its position in a two-sentence paragraph many column inches down or minutes in.
- If you encounter a report that's using this kind of spin-speak, let whoever is responsible for the story know. Call or email the reporter, the newspaper's editor, the station's News Editor and/or Assignment Editor to alert them to their mistake. Be polite,

informative, and coherent. They are probably unaware of their gaffe and may be willing to change their stance.[99]

I've hammered at the nuclear industry's disinformation through languaging tricks on *Nuclear Hotseat* from the first. They form the invisible basis of the nuclear industry's continuing sleight of hand which misdirects our attention away from their violations against people and the environment. If you can be convinced that nukes are great, we need them to combat global warming, they're safe and reliable, with no negative impact to people or the environment, there doesn't seem to be any reason to get rid of them. If Nuclear Spin-Speak remains uncontested, the nuclear industry's power to perpetuate itself will remain as invisibly powerful as radiation…

And, in my opinion, just as deadly.

CHAPTER 15

FACING MY DEMONS

It's hard to know how to end a book like this because, like ionizing radiation, the story has no ending, only a never-ending series of half-lives.

Or so I thought until early 2018, when fate, destiny, or divine intervention by the Great Karmic Fart led me to a new Facebook group: Three Mile Island Survivors. Almost 4,000 people who identified with that term had signed up as members of this private online group. I read posts where people described illnesses, losses, fears, and anger, finally reaching out after 39 years to break their sense of isolation.

And so they broke mine.

I posted on the site, first tentatively, as someone who had been there for the accident but never lived in the area. I was afraid I'd be rejected as a TMI wannabe for the insipid nature of my involvement in the accident when compared with that of people who lived there, stuck with not just the event itself but its decades of aftermath. In that way, I was like a sexual abuse survivor who tries to minimize her abuse by saying, "But it only happened to me X number of times; you had it so much worse because it happened to you YZ times."

But the admins welcomed me immediately and warmly. I posted an introduction of myself to the group, told them about *Nuclear Hotseat*, and that I produced a Three Mile Island Anniversary Special every year.

Then I learned there was to be a panel discussion near Middletown for the 39th anniversary of the accident. It would include not only some genuine experts I knew and had interviewed, but several journalists who had been involved in covering the accident at TMI as it happened.

I debated the expense of last-minute travel, the heavy hit to my adrenals that comes with traveling, my nervous resistance to facing up to TMI again, and then realized: if I did not attend, I would regret it for the rest of my life. No regrets, remember? I didn't need a cosmic Voice in my right ear to remind me. So I booked my flights, room, a rental car, dog care, allocated two full days for travel, and gave myself two days on the ground.

I was going back to TMI to face my demon.

In my Recovery days, we had a term: "Coming up on a memory." It meant we had a feeling, a deep dis-ease, that something long repressed and terrible, yet essential to our healing, was about to burst forth into consciousness. When we felt it, this early warning system would allow us to hit the hold button on the memory long enough to get to a safe space.

Then we could let it come ripping out in all its fury. We'd let the emotions rock us as the terror of abuse we had repressed into amnesia and locked away in our cells made itself known. The emotions would release the memories of what we'd experienced but had to consciously forget in order to survive, as jagged swells of feeling left us sobbing,

142

screaming, cursing God and/or our perpetrators. We needed to ride this wild pony until it spent itself completely; once started, there was no way off until we'd completely drained it of all details.

Then we would collapse, stunned to stupefication. Whatever repressed memory had revealed itself would ever after remain available to us as information, unbound by emotion. It became something we could write about, tell to others, deal with as fact separate from pain – not as an unknown, terrifying source of crippling fear and inexplicable behaviors.

With this memory release, every compensating behavior and belief we'd subconsciously created to hold our fear in place was available to be evaporated from our lives. Based on this new awareness, we could choose to release and reprogram even our most destructive habits. Food, alcohol, drugs, sexual compulsions, OCD, misplaced anger, denial of self-care – every one of those undermining behaviors could finally leave us, to be consciously replaced by self-soothing, nurturing, healing.

Sometimes, the psyche would want to cling to the old behavior a bit longer as something familiar that protected us when nothing else in our environment did. We trusted the old coping mechanisms, even if they now hurt us. But by being gentle with ourselves, by releasing the belief or behavior with gratitude and love – sometimes with prayer and ceremony – we could emerge into a larger, truer sense of who we were.

By deciding to go to Three Mile Island, I was intentionally "coming up on a memory." Big time. I wanted to know what I still held onto from that experience and finally release it from my life.

I took every opportunity to jolt my memory. In the 10

days I had to prepare, I read my journals from that time, which had remained untouched for 39 years. I produced my yearly TMI Anniversary Special for *Nuclear Hotseat*,[100] again immersing myself in the sounds and information from that terrible time:

- Archival audio of Walter Cronkite, "the most trusted newsman in America," somberly announcing the accident on his CBS national news broadcast.
- Lies by nuclear industry mouthpieces meant to reassure us, when their unconscious slip-ups and unconvincing tone let us know that they were scared, too.
- The interview I did with Mary Stamos, long-time Middletown resident who lived 6-1/2 miles from TMI. She has collected evidence of fasciation (radiation-based plant mutations) and animal mutations, and personally launched a door-to-door epidemiological study of the impact of the accident five years after it happened when she learned that the government hadn't done this yet – and wouldn't.
- An update by Eric Epstein, executive director of Three Mile Island Alert, explaining the long term consequences of the accident, including legal battles fought and lost by judicial fiat.

Every year, I re-edit the program to include new audio, so I was in it all the way, remembering the experience, feeling the pressure build, my stomach clenching as I listened to the voices from that time, that story.

My story.

Yeah, it was time for me to return.

I took three flights and arrived just after midnight on the anniversary, March 28. Because it was too late to pick up a rental car, I was unable to join activists at the annual vigil at the gates of TMI, which started at 3:57 a.m. – what some claim is the exact time the accident began.

Later that day, after I got my wheels, I drove directly to Middletown, with which I experienced an eerie familiarity. Despite the 39 years, I drove straight to Kuppy's, the little diner where I'd seen that reporter and camera operator sitting at the counter.

I again took a counter seat in order to talk with the two incredibly efficient waitresses and the cook, who is a fourth generation member of the Kuppy family. When I told them I was there "for the anniversary," nobody asked what anniversary; they all knew. I asked about their memories of the accident and they energetically shared stories of being in school and scared as their parents pulled them out of class on that first day and fled Middletown. But they each returned with their families only a short time later.

As for any health aftereffects, they shrugged and went about their business, reluctant to go into any detail or even, it seems, meet my eye. Obviously, they had all gotten on with their lives, never leaving the area. At their shared reluctance to provide personal details, I didn't pry.

However, they did share a wealth of information about the local community. I learned that the high school where the NRC press conference had taken place no longer exists. When I described the area I had been staying, one of the waitresses, Terry, said it sounded like Royalton, the neighborhood she lives in. She told me that the mini-mart – a Circle K – had closed years before and been turned into a food bank. Then she offered instructions on how to find it.

Despite zigging and zagging along the streets of Royalton, several times stopping to ask for directions, I didn't see anything that looked right. No house. No food bank. No vantage point from which to view the cooling towers. Rather than continue to search – a kind way of saying I was dragging my feet to avoid the main event – I faced the inevitable and hooked a left onto Rte. 441, the road to Three Mile Island.

The day was cloudy, with a fine drizzle. I drove cautiously, eyes alternately on the road and the Susquehanna River to my right. Suddenly, the cooling towers emerged – enormous, silent, overpowering, belching thick white steam into the air so that they were cloaked in mist, like a shy bride in her veils, unwilling to reveal herself completely for fear of exposing the truth about her sullied past and damaged reputation.

At first glimpse of the towers, my body convulsed as if kicked in the solar plexus. I gripped the steering wheel and cried out. A part of me that had been running from this memory for 39 years came in for a crash landing. Past fused with present: The cooling towers I'd remembered were still there.

I think part of me really hoped that this was all some bad *Twilight Zone* episode I'd stumbled into, that reality would snap back into something lighthearted and laughable, and I'd be another person altogether.

But I hadn't made it up. It had happened. This, now, was real.

I knew I needed to get to a safe spot and process the erupting emotions. This was no "coming up on a memory;" I was in it.

I drove past the entrance to Three Mile Island with its No Trespassing warnings and looked for a place to pull over. Ironically, the best place I could find was just down the road, the parking lot of TMI owner/operator Exelon's headquarters, right across from the reactors. Fearing criminal trespass charges – though there was absolutely no security in sight – I parked far from the building, facing the cooling towers.

One of the techniques I learned during incest recovery was the planned, controlled retriggering of PTSD by returning to "the scene of the crime" at a time and in a way that was safe. That would allow me to feel long-delayed emotions that had been suppressed and coded into my body, buried away from consciousness as too much, not safe to feel or express.

Here, now, finally, I could let it out. And I did.

The fear.

The madness.

The existential dread that not only was I about to die, but so was the entire world as we knew it.

All that emotional weight that had been holding my life in check, haunting my creativity, my career, my relationships, my self-care, my sense of self…

Alone in the car, facing those iconic cooling towers and all they represented, I let myself mourn the loss of the woman I never got to be.

Pulling together the woman I had become, I got out to take a few selfies with the local neighborhood hot spot. I'd wanted to match the vantage point from which the pictures had been taken back in 1979 and this was as close as I could find. I'd worn my *Nuclear Hotseat* logo tee shirt to match the "I Survived Three Mile Island" one I'd had on in the photos years before.

I am nothing if not symbolically harmonic.

Selfies Я Not Us. I managed a few of iffy quality, fearing all the time that Exelon Security was going to nab me at any moment. But the only criminal trespass was those reactors, defiling the environment, stealing years, health, and life, forever polluting the future as they have been for the last 39 years and even before that, from their first day of operation.

Exelon ignored me. Obviously they did not care about some aging hippie taking anniversary snapshots with their pride and joy as a backdrop.

I drove back to the entrance to TMI, parked on a side street, and walked past the No Trespass warning signs, looking for a better shot than those feeble selfies. The cooling towers were visible just a little way up the river.

A young man in a service truck had stopped at the edge of the No Trespassing zone and gotten out to check something outside his vehicle. I ran over to him and asked if he'd take some pictures of me with the cooling towards in the background. He happily obliged.[101] As I explained why I was there, he told me that he worked for a company that serviced some of the non-nuclear equipment on site. The area he worked in was next to the containment vessel and he said he always felt uneasy as he did his job. He was early 30's and married, but had no children yet. He knew the basic dangers of radiation exposure and his proximity with the reactors concerned him, though not enough to look for another line of work.

I asked if he'd heard of the event taking place the next night, but he hadn't. And from his attitude, I sensed he didn't want to.[102]

Photos accomplished[103] and emotions drained, I drove back to Royalton and resumed the search for my friends' house. With the help of a local security cop, I found a subdivision of duplexes that looked like what I'd stayed in, but I wasn't sure which one.

With perfect timing, a resident pulled into his driveway next to where I'd parked. As he stepped out of his truck, I went over. I told him why I was there. He'd only lived there about 10 years and had no direct knowledge of the meltdown or my friends. So I quizzed him on two architectural details I'd remembered about my friends' duplex: Did the windows consist of a single sheet of glass with some kind of tape or etching to make it look like multiple panes? And was his bathtub a solid fiberglass insert and not a freestanding tub? Yes to both.

OK, I was in the right neighborhood, even if I had not yet found the house.

I walked around the area. Looking for help locating the old Circle K/food bank, I went into a city-run senior center just up the road. No one could help me find my target, but I took advantage of the opportunity to interview a few of the people there. Most had lived in Middletown when the accident happened but expressed no concern over it. One woman interrupted her card game to joke that she'd sent her dog away, but she and her husband stayed put. Another woman's office emptied out of more than 400 workers on the first day, but she stayed on at the call center because she was new to the job and needed the money. Others avoided me or denied that anything of importance had happened.

But then one woman called me over to where she sat with her husband. They talked quietly of the death of their son at only 54, after a 15 year battle with cancer. Another elderly woman said her brother died of cancer and she blamed "the Three Mile," but had no proof to back up her belief. They kept their voices low as they spoke, as though they were doing something shameful to break silence on their fears and suspicions.

I drove back to my motel and collapsed for the evening. My major activity consisted of using Facebook to alert friends and *Nuclear Hotseat* followers of my progress and post a few pictures of me posing with the cooling towers.

The pics provoked quite the reaction. Most were a variation on the theme of, "ARE YOU NUTS?!? GET AWAY!" As I pushed the Like button to acknowledge that I'd seen their message, I had to smile. Too late! The time to warn me was 39 years ago… not that I would have listened.

Next day, March 29 – the anniversary of my walk to Middletown where I'd breathed so deeply of the Pennsylvania springtime air – I returned to Three Mile Island. I'd seen a turnoff to a public boat launch at the river less than a mile downstream from the towers. In the dreary weather, it was as deserted as I'd hoped.

"Coming up on a memory." I knew what I needed to do. Alone in nature, I gave myself over to the deepest level of those feelings, lived them and made them current, real. I cried as I'd cried during the incest recovery retreats. I found a thick stick and beat the ground in rage, cursing everyone from Einstein to Exelon until the stick broke. I invented ceremony on the spot and shouted at those cooling towers that they and what they stood for no longer had any power over me. I threw rocks and sticks into the river as symbols of my rage and pledged myself to doing whatever I can to take those suckers down, and with them, the industry they stand for.

I stayed for over an hour, riding the swells of emotion until I eventually came down to where I could trust myself to drive. I usually take a small memento from places in nature where I've had a significant emotional release or memorable experience. A rock. A shell. A leaf. An acorn.

Not this time. Not this close to TMI.

On the drive back to Middletown, everything I saw enraged me. A dairy farm right across the road from TMI selling fresh milk. Houses with kids' bikes on the lawn. Pets roaming around. Easter decorations. All of it so *normal*. I wanted to scream, "Get out! Get out! What are you still doing here? Don't you know what you're facing?"

But they probably don't – and besides, where is there to go?

I returned to Kuppy's. Over perfect eggs and hash browns, I thanked Terry for her help the day before and asked few more questions about the location of the food bank. Taking another slow drive through Royalton, I finally found it, though the building looked different than I'd remembered. I sighted down the road that ran beside it. Even with misty rain obscuring the view, I could see the cooling towers, just across some train tracks, down the river.

"About a mile. That way." That's what the man in the mini-mart had said as he pointed, 39 years ago. Maybe it was closer to a mile and a half, or even two miles, but after all this time, it seems inconsequential to quibble.

From the place where I spotted the cooling towers, I turned 180 degrees, looking for my friends' house. That's when saw a short dead end in the subdivision that I'd not noticed the day before. With an eerie sense of… not déjà vu, but of history re-entered, I walked a short distance and stood in front of the house.

That house. The one with the front door I had swung open to hear the bullhorn and the upstairs window I slammed shut. The house without a basement. The place my friends had lived for only three months because they'd married six months before and he'd gotten a job as an airplane mechanic at the Harrisburg airport and they'd just moved in. The place where I landed when I made my mad dash from the break-up of what I referred to as "an obsessive non-relationship" in Los Angeles, only to end up in a small, quiet town in Pennsylvania that, for a little while, turned into hell.

I walked back the way I'd come, stopped at the corner... and there was the same view of TMI that I'd seen from next to the food bank.

This was where I'd been. This is where I'd stood 39 years before. This is where my life slid into the *Twilight Zone* and, in some essential way, had never left. Only now, right now, yes now, in this very moment, at this very place, did part of me shift back into alignment with that young woman I used to be. The one scared out of her mind and her wits, who could no longer be who she'd been and did not yet know who she was going to turn into.

As I stood there, balanced between memory and presence, feeling feelings for which I still do not have words, I allowed myself to remember and finally own who that young woman – who I'd – really been: my insensitivity to others, which at the time I labeled "bravado," but it was really arrogance. My selfishness and the clumsy ignorance-in-action that tore apart four relationships at a single go. The ego that convinced me that TMI was some karmic, cosmic punishment for my sins, divine retribution aimed at me for my personal behaviors that incidentally leaked out into the surrounding community, the country, the world, in radiation and an ongoing nuclear nightmare.

But all that was the fabrication of a distorted mind, its coping mechanisms created to deal with emotional pressures of which I was not yet consciously aware. The truth is, that young woman who was me was deeply damaged long before TMI, and doing the best she could to get through life, despite the fact that her resulting rationales sounded crazy even to her.

Perpetration is as perpetration does, and while my earliest abuse remained repressed in amnesia for another six years, Three Mile Island assaulted my body in much the same way as my incest perpetrators – silently, invisibly, with easy deniability. And I, naturally, responded as an incest survivor would – with isolation, self-blame, grandiosity, and emotional repression in an effort to blot the experience from my mind. In the process, I spent decades denying myself much that was good in life, and learned to assume that failure was my fate and "almost" was my unavoidable destiny.

Enough. She'd punished herself enough. *I* had punished *myself* enough. As I learned from Spiritual Psychology, our negative behaviors are held in place by the self-judgments we hold against ourselves. Invoking a patterned emotional release exercise I'd used throughout my Masters degree training, I forgave the judgments I'd held against my younger self. I released the emotional bondage of the past. I lay my burden down. I accepted the Truth that I was doing the best I could with what I had, and the time had come to let it all go.

It was finally enough. *I* was finally enough.

I took pictures, of course. That's what cell phones are for. I included several shots of the street signs so I could never misplace the location of this hallowed ground, ever again.

Then I packed up my psyche and left.

I had a panel discussion to attend.

CHAPTER 16

THE UNREPORTED CONSEQUENCES OF TMI

The panel discussion was held at a country club in Dillsburg, 24 miles from Middletown. I arrived early and had a good time catching up with two former *Nuclear Hotseat* interviewees who were on the panel: Cindy Folkers, Radiation and Health Specialist for Beyond Nuclear, and Heidi Hutner, PhD, who carries the unwieldy title of Director of Sustainability Studies & Associate Dean at the School of Marine & Atmospheric Sciences at Stony Brook University. Heidi and I had never met in person, but we'd developed close ties through an energetic Facebook correspondence.

Also present were several members of Three Mile Island Alert, including Scott Portzline, who'd been a strong supporter of *Nuclear Hotseat* and a tech wiz who'd helped me out with many audio challenges. Mary Stamos, a founder of TMIA, attended despite a recent spate of ill health, wearing a T-shirt with the unmistakable message: "NO is a Nuclear Reaction." She brought photos from her

39 years of research into mutations of plants and animals in the area.

The mood in the room was nervous, squirrely, a combination of the organizers' pre-event jitters, last-minute tech troubleshooting, and what I perceived as the community members' fear at what they might learn and anger at what they already knew. For some questionable legal reasons, I'd been asked not to interview any of the attendees that night, so I engaged in brief conversations and collected follow-up contact numbers.

I primarily sought out the reporters who'd covered the accident. I introduced myself as both a journalist covering the event and someone who'd been there when it happened. With these dual credentials, I made a good connection with each of them.

The panel. Despite the fact that I'd immersed myself in nuclear issues every week for almost seven years, scouring the internet for verifiable news stories and interviewing world experts at length, I was not prepared for what I learned that night.

The reporters began, relating their personal stories.[104] Cameraman Frank Goldstein had been in a helicopter taking aerial footage of the cooling towers when he received a frantic message: "Get out! They just released more radiation!" Before the panel started, Frank had confided to me that he suffers from a heart condition, "one that is consistent with someone who had rheumatic fever – only I never had rheumatic fever." He also said that Kuppy's deserves an award, because, "when everyone else fled, they stayed behind to feed the reporters."

Frank gets together with other Philadelphia-area reporters four times a year, many of whom covered Three Mile Island, more than half of whom are seriously ill.[105]

Veteran radio personality Dan Steele, beloved in central Pennsylvania after more than 40 years on the air, brought the heart of the event into stark focus. He admitted at the start that he suffers from Post Traumatic Stress Disorder, caused by a combination of an incident in Vietnam and his experiences with TMI.

I almost stopped breathing. This was the first time I heard anyone other than myself speak of Three Mile Island has having induced PTSD.

Dan had covered the accident on the first day. He believed the assurances of his contacts at MetEd, the utility company that ran the reactors, that everything had been taken care of and there was nothing to worry about. On that basis, two days after the accident began, Dan flew to San Antonio for a long-planned job interview. When he landed, the station general manager nervously asked him if he didn't want to get back to Middletown.

"Why?" Dan responded. "It was handled two days ago."

Then the GM filled Dan in on the latest information that has surfaced while he was in flight: more radiation released and evacuation "recommended" for people within five miles. Dan's wife had safely evacuated to New Jersey. The world's journalists were descending on his home turf to cover the big story. Shouldn't he be there?

Dan took the next plane out. He expected his connecting flight out of Chicago to be empty, but found it jammed with reporters and camera crews. At Harrisburg Airport, no cabs would come that close to the reactors to pick anyone up. Dan managed to get a ride from a colleague to his eerily dark, abandoned neighborhood. Calling his station, WKBO, he spoke with news director Mike Pintek – the only person left on site. When Dan asked Pintek how he was doing, the man admitted he was "ready to meet his maker."

Dan added that Mike Pintek now has cancer.

As he told his story, Dan regularly and unembarrassedly choked up, stopping to compose himself before continuing. The raw nature of his wound, visible even after all these years, spoke volumes to the continuing emotional impact of Three Mile Island on those who went through it. His bravery in allowing us to see what happened to him, what is still happening, resonated through the room, and I heard others gasping and muffling their own sobs.

I may have been one of them.

It struck me that, like sexual abuse victims, this is a community that has been perpetrated against, physically and emotionally damaged and put down by corporate interests with an agenda. Its people had never been given permission to feel or share or rage against what had been done to them by that nuclear reactor and the industry it represents. Like a child growing up in a family with rampant sexual abuse, they'd learned to obey the taboo against talking honestly and directly about what happened to them and their loved ones. I had seen it in the seniors who virtually whispered their fears of familial cancer deaths because of TMI, and the Kuppy's crew who chatted about their high school-era fears but avoided speaking of any possibly related health problems with family, neighbors, friends. Cover it up. Pretend. Nothing important happened.

"Nobody died at Three Mile Island." (We'll get back to that.)

Here, in this room, the veil lifted for the local residents. Permission to feel was granted... and more was about to be revealed.

Cindy Folkers has been studying radiation impact on health for over 25 years. As she started, she clearly told everyone that she is not a scientist or a researcher, but sources her work from original research data and interprets the numbers so normal people can understand what they mean. Cindy spoke of sub-clinical damage from radiation exposure, things that don't register as a disease but still can cause subtle damage to our bodies, damage that plays out over years and perhaps generations.

What she said hit me so hard, I heard nothing after the words, "sub-clinical damage." Was it possible that, at the root of my adrenal problems, was more than an emotional response to TMI? I couldn't wrap my head around it fast enough to retain anything else she was saying. I couldn't even take notes. But Cindy and I had a breakfast planned for the next day; I'd be able to ask her privately.

Heidi Hutner talked of how the US built suburbs around major cities so people in this perimeter had a chance of surviving a nuclear blast aimed at urban centers. She paralleled her recent work at Rocky Flats in Colorado and the Hanford Nuclear Reservation in Washington state with the situation around TMI – the building of beautiful homes, new schools, open parklands, and the illusion of The Good Life at what are still dangerously radioactive sites. All these actions were meant to normalize our perceptions of the nuclear dangers of the area.[106] Heidi is both writing a book and producing a film about nuclear industry devastation and information manipulation under the title, *Accidents Can Happen.*

The real surprise for me was a local endocrinologist, Dr. Renu Joshi. She'd been trained in medical school to pay close attention to anyone who had been exposed to radiation and provide regular follow-up exams, though in most cases this applied to patients who'd had their tonsils irradiated in childhood. But Dr. Joshi noticed many anomalies in thyroid cancer cases in her Mechanicsburg-area practice, only 65 miles away from TMI. Unable to find published data to help her understand what was going on, she did research on her own patients. Among her discoveries:

- Out of 300 thyroid cancer cases within her practice, she found 20 to 22 incidents of high-to-medium risk thyroid cancer. These cases appeared at double the national average – 10.2% of her patients as opposed to 5% average for the country.
- The cases she treated were more aggressive than most cases of thyroid cancer and did not respond to the usual treatment.
- The average age of onset of thyroid cancer among her patients was 42, while the national average is 47. Local residents were getting sick five years earlier than their non-TMI counterparts.
- Almost three-quarters of these more aggressive thyroid cancer cases occurred in people who had lived within 15 miles of TMI when the accident happened.

Dr. Joshi's findings are now being peer reviewed for publication and she is continuing her research, which appears to prove that TMI has had a definite effect upon thyroid cancer incidence and severity in the Middletown area.

Mary Stamos of TMI Alert presented photos of plant fasciation and animal mutations from her extensive collection – dandelions with 3′ long leaves, flowers blooming out of the center of other flowers, a two-headed calf, more. A Q&A brought audience members and other journalists to the mic, where local concerns were given voice, accompanied by nodding heads and occasional shouts of outrage from the audience.

After the panel ended, as the attendees dispersed, I hung with the reporters, thanking them for their stories, promising follow-up and interviews to enlarge my coverage of TMI. Then there were the obligatory selfies with Cindy and Heidi, lots of hugs, and quiet conversations with the organizers, thanking them for what they had done.

That night, too overwhelmed to process, I fell into an exhausted, dreamless sleep.

Next morning, packed and ready to go, I met Cindy Folkers for breakfast. We'd seen each other on the run through years of various anti-nuclear events, but never had time for more than a 90 second, "Hi! Great to see you! Love your latest (show/post/article). Oops, they're starting the next session, gotta run, see ya!" with a hug at either end. I'd never before had the luxury of talking with her at length and not being constrained by the parameters of the interview. We lingered over coffee, just two women passionate about the same issue, knowing many of the same people, sharing the intimacy of a conversation where we didn't have to provide footnotes in order to be understood.

Cindy reaffirmed that there is more damage created by exposure to ionizing radiation than the diseases we recognize as connected, such as cancers, heart conditions, birth defects, auto-immune diseases. "There are what are called 'subclinical health problems,'" she said, "not all diagnosable diseases, but conditions, including 'syndromes,' that can come from a radiation-induced problem with the DNA." Possible problems she mentioned include allergies, autism, infertility, a wider gamut of auto-immune illnesses, failure to thrive... Could that possibly include my adrenal gland issues?

Cindy went on. "Sub-clinical problems can be created at the genetic level, not just by direct exposure to the radiation. This means it is passed on to future generations as a recessive gene. That is why the problem does not necessarily show up in the first generation after the accident, unless two people with this recessive gene mate, in which case the genetic problem becomes dominant and expresses itself. Because it is embedded in our genes, there is currently no turning back, no 'correcting' it. This is a permanent change in the gene pool."

I felt like I was sliding sideways into an alternative reality. I'd blamed my adrenal problems on the emotional trauma of having been at TMI and the years of stress that resulted. In essence, I accepted part of the blame for my declining adrenal function – my tiredness, the time lost by staying in bed, napping, turning down invitations to do things I wanted to do with people I wanted to do them with because I lacked the energy. Familial echoes had played a subliminal infinity loop in the back of my mind: "Lazy." "Unmotivated." "Underachiever." "Loser." Decades of self-blame, self-shaming, beating myself up for not having the overweening energy I'd experienced throughout childhood and early adult years –

And now, here was Cindy, cautiously choosing her words to be scientifically accurate in reporting her research, and bowling me over. In essence, she was telling me that in all likelihood, the exposure I'd experienced primarily on that second day, walking into Middletown and waiting for a bus to Harrisburg, the one time I was up close and personal with the radioactive Pennsylvania springtime air, is what might have done it to me – created some sub-clinical ding to my DNA. Over years of cellular duplication and replacement, this is what had impacted my health far beyond any emotional reaction.

Sitting across from Cindy in that overly cheerful coffee shop, I felt both vindicated and devastated. Finally, I knew the truth. I didn't like it, but at least I knew it.

And if my adrenal exhaustion stemmed from some subtle TMI-induced damage to my DNA, I'd been right in my decision to not have children.

Wrung out by these not-yet-digested insights, I left Cindy with another hug to deal with three flights, stupid Über, steadily worsening stomach cramps, and TMI x 2 – meaning Too Much Information about Three Mile Island. I got home, reclaimed my dog, and crashed, barely leaving my bed for two full days.

My processing had just begun.

CHAPTER 17

CLOSURE... AND BEYOND

My trip to Three Mile Island gave me a sense of closure. I stared my demon down and did not blink. I saw the cooling towers, found the house where I'd stayed, confirmed my memories of that time, learned the truth of what I'd been exposed to, and what probably resulted. More importantly, I found a community of people who shared my concerns. Theirs are compounded by continuing proximity to the source of their original exposure, which provides regular if not daily re-traumatization.[107] But it's oddly comforting to know that there's at least one place on earth where I can say "TMI" and everyone will know what I'm talking about.

Back in Los Angeles, I produced *Nuclear Hotseat* #355, [108] wherein I related highlights from my trip, including audio from the senior center and the panel discussion. It already ranks as one of my most downloaded episodes. In the shows I've produced since then, I bring up TMI at every opportunity – not just as my boilerplate earn-the-right mention at the top of each episode, but as a talking point or pivot in an interview to focus whatever we're talking about onto what happened there, what's still happening.

So what actually happened at Three Mile Island?

- According to TMI officials, the NRC and the government, no radiation readings on the releases were ever made because the monitors used to measure them malfunctioned. I always thought this was because they were supplied by the lowest bidder and when the emergency happened, the units didn't work. What I didn't learn until after Fukushima, when I watched video of a lecture given by Arnie Gundersen, was that the radiation release so exceeded the design basis of the meters that in essence the equipment "fried" early on the first day. There has never been an accurate measurement of the radiation released at Three Mile Island – or if there was, it's never been released to the public.[109]

- Evacuation of the surrounding area was justified yet ignored three different times on the first day, March 28.[110] Engineers in the control room at Three Mile Island debated calling the governor for an evacuation the morning of the accident and the discussion was recorded by a Dictaphone machine; whether left on intentionally or accidentally I do not know. At one point someone asks, "Shouldn't we evacuate?" After a long pause, another man says, "No, I don't think that's a good idea."[111] In that way, in that moment, with that single sentence, my entire life was changed forever without my knowledge or consent. Ultimately, that was the moment all my children died.

- March 29, the second day, as I walked into Middletown to get some interviews, Three Mile Island released a large radioactive plume.[112] I have problems reading maps, so I used to think the plume blew in the opposite direction from where I stayed with friends. I've only recently revisited that information and discovered that I was to the north and slightly east of Three Mile Island, quite possibly inside the radiation plume on the first day. Fortunately, I stayed inside writing that entire day except for my brief trip to the mini-mart in the early evening. If I'd been out and walking around, I would most likely have been exposed to a much larger amount of radioactivity and quite possibly not survived long enough to wake up, become active, and write this book.

- The U.S. government did not even start testing the accident's impact on the health of the local population until five years after it took place – the exact same time-delay tactic taken after Hiroshima and Nagasaki. At that point, more than half the people who'd been living near the reactors in 1979 had moved away and thus were never studied. No attempt has ever been made to find them, nor was any attempt ever made by government officials to tease out relevant data from local hospital records during those first five years.

- There were out-of-court financial settlements paid by TMI reactor designers Babcock and Wilcox and operator Metropolitan Edison-General Public Utilities to specific individuals who were rumored to have experienced the worst, most direct, immediate, and incontrovertible damage as a result of the radiation releases. Of course, these settlements came with a gag order, so the people involved cannot talk about their cases and the amount of their settlements is not publically known.[113]

- While nuclear proponents loudly parrot the phrase, "No one died at Three Mile Island," Pennsylvania Cancer Registry statistics from 1985 to 2008 show that the highest rate of thyroid cancer in the United States is with 50 miles of that nuclear reactor.[114, 115]

Three Mile Island has been dismissed for too long, too thoroughly, too effectively by the industry that back in 1979 was just starting to invent the playbook it now follows after every nuclear "Oops!" As a result, most people – even many activists – assume the "partial" meltdown[116] was really no big deal. After all, as the nuclear industry and its supporters have drummed into our heads for 39 years, "Nobody died at Three Mile Island."

Stop right there. Remember spin-speak? The nuclear industry has learned to semantically manipulate language and embed their lies so they appear to be the truth. This is a brilliant example, because what they say is, literally, 100% true: Nobody died at Three Mile Island. That is, nobody died AT the Three Mile Island Nuclear Generating Station, located on Three Mile Island in Londonderry Township, Pennsylvania, on the Susquehanna River, just south of Harrisburg, Pennsylvania. Nobody, not one single person, ever keeled over and dropped dead AT the site of that nuclear reactor meltdown.

BUT – did people die FROM Three Mile Island? FROM the radiation released by that accident and, over time, what it did to their health, DNA, ability to conceive a child and carry it full term, the birth defects, cancer, heart disease, auto-immune diseases, and a whole raft of still-being-discovered sub-clinical syndromes?

HELL, YES.

Don't take my word for it. Look at the work of epidemiologist Dr. Steven Wing,[117, 118] Cindy Folkers,[119] Dr. Helen Caldicott,[120] nuclear engineer and safety consultant Arnie Gundersen,[121] epidemiologist Joseph Mangano,[122] British independent consultant on radioactivity in the environment Dr. Ian Fairlie,[123] and -- when her work becomes available – look at what Dr. Renu Joshi has discovered about local thyroid cancer rates. The nuclear industry and its paid publicity whores have tried to make you look away from these truth-tellers, the ones who examined the scientific data, teased out the real story, had it peer-reviewed, published it, and then tried to get someone, anyone, everyone to pay attention.

Scientific data doesn't do it for you? How about anecdotal stories? Read the posts on the Facebook Three Mile Island Survivors page,[124] where local residents are finally breaking silence on their fears, the rampant cancers and other illnesses in their bodies, in their families, their loved ones who are dying, and those already lost.

Still not enough? Look at material posted on the Three Mile Island Alert website.[125] On the landing page, which has links to information on several nuclear reactors, click on Three Mile Island and then, next screen, Health Studies. That's where you'll find a summary of the medically researched truth about the health impact of that accident and its radiation releases. One of these reports cites more than a dozen footnoted health studies that contradict the nuclear industry's party line.[126] Elsewhere on the TMIA site, read about what legal cases have been filed by the victims, won, and then been lost on appeal in front of judges who were either industry-friendly, mis-informed, science-ignorant, stuck with applying an ill-conceived or badly written law, or any combination of the above.

A cursory review of these online sites will reveal that all information not already contaminated and spun by the nuclear industry points to Three Mile Island as having been devastating to the health and wellbeing of those who lived through the accident, as well as their descendants. And every other nuclear facility, be it a reactor, weapons manufacturing site, uranium mine, radioactive waste dump, or the transport routes between them, does the exact same thing – invisibly assault the health and genetic future of people and the environment. All it will take is a microscopic crack in an embrittled containment vessel or thin-walled dry storage cask,[127] the failure of a critical piece of reactor equipment, loss of offsite power that outlives the limited fuel supply dedicated for use in emergency cooling generators, or that most common of all nuclear weak links: human error. Any one of those could start another TMI, Fukushima... or worse.

And nobody except a few activists, scientists, engineers, researchers, and podcasters seem to be concerned enough to pay this any attention.

The nukesters may think they'll continue to get away with everything they've been getting away with since the beginning of the nuclear age. If something catastrophic happens, top honchos are among those who figure they can escape to their already-purchased former sheep farms in New Zealand. They clearly trust that *On the Beach* was right and southern hemisphere re-homing will allow them to escape the worst when the northern hemisphere goes up in a nuclear Armageddon – or just passively contaminates itself to lifeless hell.

Or perhaps they will join with other members of the monied elite who plan to stash their lives, genes, and the genetic future of their descendants in old U.S. missile silos converted into billionaire condos.[128] They may think they will reap the benefits of cushy survival and live to re-establish life on Earth on their terms, but in my experience, the Law of Unintended Consequences is adjudicated by a Spirit with a wicked sense of humor. At minimum, who will their children be if they never see the sky? What kind of a world will be left outside those silos/bunkers for their descendants to inherit? And how dare we – how dare anyone – destroy this magnificent web of life for something as false, transient, and ultimately meaningless as money, let alone money made by splitting the atom to boil water?

Anyone in the nuclear industry reading this book for a bit of a chuckle – and I know I have lurkers on *Nuclear Hotseat* so I'm willing to bet at least a few of you bought a copy – do you really think you're immune to the consequences of your actions? Stop for a moment and consider the field in which you work and its impact through the lens of just one of its many proven disease consequences:

- Cancer used to be a rare disease, but since 1945 and the start of the nuclear age, its numbers have soared. Current statistics from the American Cancer Society point to cancer being *expected* to show up in one of two women, one of three men.[129] And cancer rates are even higher for those who live or lived in proximity to nuclear reactors.[130]
- We know beyond any doubt that exposure to radiation, even so-called "low level" radiation, causes damage to cells that can lead to cancer. That's why pregnant women are warned not to have x-rays,

so the rapidly growing fetus will not be irrevocably damaged by the radiation.

- Think about your own life. Can you honestly say that you do not know a single person who has or had cancer? What is the cancer incidence in your childhood neighborhood, your current region, your family, yourself?
- What makes you think these facts are unrelated to the work you do?

In Recovery terms, if you work in the nuclear industry, you're either a perpetrator – one who commits the offense against others, or an enabler – one who helps the perpetrator get away with it.

The thing about perpetrators is that they were invariably perpetrated against in childhood, which is how they learned this dominance behavior in the first place. It makes me wonder about those people who so staunchly commit, defend, and promote nuclear perpetration: What happened to them? Who did what and how old were they when it started? After they were hurt, did they ever get help? Or did they just get mean, isolated, depressed, shut down, and/or so angry that they lost connection with empathy and compassion and didn't care who or what they hurt in return? Is that why they have no problem promoting this deadly technology, down to writing press releases, slick acronyms, and lies of both commission and omission in order to promote nuclear perpetration and its expansionist plans around the world? Is that how they can rationalize away any nagging doubts about the impact of what they're doing, because, "Hey, [insert industry-approved spin-speak talking point here] and ya gotta pay the mortgage, ya know?" Or did they just "eat the baby" in order to gain their own sickly corner of power in the world so their personal perpetrators couldn't do it to them again?

No matter how the nuclear industry, its apologists, or any of the world's governments spin their information or bury it under left-brained jargon, nothing will stop that already-released radiation from doing what it is going to do: barrel through whatever its particles invisibly, sub-microscopically encounter, and leave a path of destruction in its wake. If even one radioactive particle gets inside us – if we breathe in a single "speck," swallow one with food or water, get it in a break in our skin – it attacks us from the inside out, up close and personal with our internal organs, at the cellular level, down to our DNA. And once radiation damages our DNA – the key that controls the ongoing, eternal fractal that is human life – nothing will ever be the same.

So the real question is: how long will it take before we have inescapably seeded the entire biosphere, Earth and its atmosphere, with enough radioactive contamination to guarantee our inevitable obliteration as a species? Might it have happened already? Is it now? Or now? How about NOW???

We don't even need to explode a nuclear bomb to get there. Radiation leaks from reactors, "permitted" releases,[131] the accumulated radioactive debris we have stockpiled with no way to safely store or decontaminate it, the particles from all 2,121 atmospheric explosions that have ever taken place[132] circling the globe in the jet stream, ready to rain out onto any place anywhere any time – all of it available to contaminate people and the environment in an ongoing barrage of radioactivy.

In this way, the nuclear industry invisibly wages atomic World War III upon us all.

This is a planetary crisis, kept hidden by people who seem to value money more than life or, at best, who do not see or understand the apocalyptic nature of what they are doing. Why? Profit, power, luxury, and an easier life are hard to turn one's back on. We've been trained by advertising, media, and un-reality TV shows to drool over "stuff," venerate money and what it can buy over the more humble human values, and so far there's no 12-step program for Recovery from money and power addiction, no Greed Anonymous[133]

Yet it is as deadly as any drug, if not more so. When John D. Rockefeller was the richest man in the world, a reporter asked him, "How much money is enough?" Rockefeller answered, "Just a little bit more."

That is the answer of an addict.

We can't expect the nuclear perpetrators to fix the problem while they're comfortably nestled in the same thinking that created it, especially when they're so richly rewarded for their choices. And a world that envies all the power, glitzy perks, and bright shiny objects money can buy yearns to emulate this financial status, join the "big boys" with their big bang power toys. Thus third world countries keep jumping on the nuclear bandwagon, not seeing the inevitable fall off into the abyss of unending radioactive nuclear waste that lurks just a little ways down that road.[134]

So in essence, humanity is screwed...

Unless.

In quantum physics – the study of the movement of particles at the smallest atomic/sub-atomic level possible – a "quantum leap" is not some enormous instantaneous change, but the smallest possible change that extrapolates out over time and distance to *become* an enormous change. Perhaps we have already taken such a profound quantum leap into a radiation-contaminated world that ultimately, as this plays out over a brief number of generations, we-as-people will not survive.

But this concept could also mean that small changes, made in as many places as possible, as quickly as possible, could possibly, eventually derail this drive towards planetary destruction and turn the ship around.

That's where We the People and grassroots activism come in. Those of us who have become aware of unremediated nuclear dangers have to push for a saner path while there's still a sliver of time in which to act. In this era of political reawakening, as the nuclear industry's egregious and long-lasting transgressions become more widely known, and genuine renewables – solar, wind, geothermal, hydroelectric, tidal, and more – have progressed to where they can take up the energy slack faster and for a lot less money, there is no reason why we cannot mobilize the masses and stop the nuclear industry once again – this time for good.

The way to do this is simple to conceive, if challenging to achieve. Step One would be to shut down all reactors to stop the creation of any new radioactive waste, especially plutonium-containing "spent" fuel rods. Boost renewables, using government funds earmarked for the nuclear industry to instead underwrite solar panels on every building, windmills where possible, and retrain nuke industry workers to use their skills in service to these alternatives.

Beyond that, there's the problem of what to do with the decades of poisonous radioactive waste that has already been created. Engineers, doctors, physicists, and activists of all kinds have told me bluntly that neutralizing radiation will not work without creating vastly larger amounts of radioactive material.

But what if it can be done, only we haven't figured it out yet?

I may be grasping at non-existent straws here, but I have to believe there must be some students, groups, and/or professors at, say, MIT, Stanford, Cal Tech, University of Illinois, or some other engineering institution, good minds that could get together in a cooperative "garage band" kind of way. They could hold the physics equivalent of a jam session, and in the process, cook up a breakthrough technology that would render ionizing radiation harmless. Maybe they could form teams and compete in a Nuclear Science Bowl: MIT vs. Stanford, any or all of the California state universities vs. the Big Ten colleges. Maybe the surprise winner would come from out of an inner city school where some discarded, discounted, sexually abused immigrant savant with dark skin from a third world country – undoubtedly female – accidentally receives a Jaime Escalante-level education,[135] and then bootstraps the skills she developed to survive in her hostile environment into turning our collective nuclear death sentence around.

Or maybe we could break the mold and instead of a competition, make it an International Nuclear Science Cooperation. Have groups around the world meet in monthly Skype or Zoom conference calls with dedicated websites to exchange information. Make the think tank international until someone cracks the code and discovers what the fictional Mork from Ork on the TV show *Mork and Mindy* called "Nuke-Away," the product used on his home planet to neutralize radiation from nuclear accidents.[136] ("It comes in pine scent or that exciting new fragrance, Fusion. It takes the worry out of being radioactive!").

To support this drive to a nuclear-radiation-free future will take money, lots of it. Imagine if Warren Buffett, Bill Gates, Richard Branson, Jeff Bezos, and a few of their venture capitalist cronies pooled their lunch money to create a billion dollar prize for whoever could devise a working model of something that would neutralize radiation. They would need to provide a structured reward schedule, with ever-increasing monetary support for teams and individuals hitting provable benchmarks, leading to a successful scalable model. This money/rewards model would also help keep schools and tech brainiacs engaged, especially if the inventers would be guaranteed the right to participate financially in their own patents so that the resulting world-changing technology couldn't be "Tesla'ed" – bought up and locked away by moneyed, corporate, and/or political interests. Make the technology available through licensing so that in addition to satisfied investors, successful team members and their sponsoring school(s) would reap the rewards and could ultimately end up richer than Warren Buffet, Bill Gates, Richard Branson, and Jeff Bezos combined.[137]

Instead, to the best of my knowledge and research, neither government, industry, education, nor philanthropy is throwing money at the problem. Even venture capitalists have turned a blind eye towards developing this potentially multi-trillion dollar technology, and it's not likely to turn up on an episode of *Shark Tank*. For all we know, some future Einstein or Tesla with the seeds of a solution already in mind is languishing at some university as a teacher's aide with crippling student loans and a side job nights at a 7/Eleven, unable to pursue her research for lack of funding.

Is such a technology even possible? Don't ask me; I told you I'm not a scientist or an engineer. But how dare we assume the answer is "no" if we haven't tried everything possible to pursue it? If the mind can conceive it, I believe we can achieve it. The questions remain: Do we have the awareness? The skills? The will? The time? The leadership? And if not – WHY THE HELL NOT????? How dare we, every one of us, not do everything in our power to find out?

And don't say it's not your problem. If you are a human being alive on the earth, just say these words out loud, right now: "It's up to me. If not me, who? If not now, when?"[138]

So I say: Ignore the naysayers, the perpetrators, nuclear shills and propagandists, the sell-out former environmentalists, the sneering left-brainers, echo chamber op-ed whores, and Russian social media bots who will do everything possible to convince you that they know best and all this nuclear worry is "alarmist"[139] bullshit. Those folks are representatives of the modern evils that Buffy Sainte Marie warned us about in her lyric to "Suffer the Children":

> "Down in the heart of town
> the Devil dresses up
> He keeps his nails clean.
> Did you think he'd be the boogey-man?"[140]

It's well-dressed, clean-nailed, overweeningly over-confident, well-paid nuclear industry wonks who will not admit that maybe, just maybe, even with luxury underground bunkers and militia–protected fiefdoms in New Zealand, that nobody, not even they, will get out of this one alive.

We know the word for murder is homicide. The murder of a parent is patricide – fratricide for a father, matricide for a mother. The murder of a king or queen? Regicide.

So what is the proper term for the murder of a biosphere? A planet? The web of life? Might it be Terracide? Ecocide? Mass suicide? Insanity? Nuclear radiation doesn't care if your politics are red, blue, purple, or any other color; the language you speak; the God you worship – or don't; your racial or ethnic heritage; who you voted for; what you weigh, wear, drive, or how much money you've got in the bank. With the single-minded simplicity of Frankenstein's monster, particles released from radioactive elements know just one thing: "I go this way. I go through whatever is in my way. I will not be stopped. I do not care what I destroy."

Failing action, what will be destroyed by nuclear radiation is us.

I hate having these awarenesses. I want my life to return to what it was before Fukushima, Chernobyl, Three Mile Island. I want my ignorance back, damn it! But a cherry once popped does not grow back, literally or figuratively. I can't look away from what I've come to think of as our pending, inevitable, species-wide planetary disaster. And having come to such a stark analysis and bleak conclusion, I must share the insights I've gained to see if I can help turn this around, or I will simply burst.

Remember, I didn't ask for this. I never wanted to be some nuclear science experiment. I was just a person with a screwed up life, without power or influence in the world, who found herself stuck one mile from a malfunctioning nuclear reactor and freaked the fuck out. This has been the story of what happened to me since then. If the nuclear industry and its propagandists and apologists don't like what I'm saying, it's their own damned fault for having done what they did to me in the first place.

Not personally, of course. Nothing personal.

And yet it's all too personal. Think not? Just ask my kids.

Without my experience at Three Mile Island, I wouldn't be paying any attention to this obscure subject matter, and certainly not giving up so much of my life as well as the writing of plays and musicals because a more important use of my creativity made itself known. I was recruited to this issue, without my consent, by forces beyond my control. Three Mile Island stole the life I would have had and left me with the pieces that I've turned into this.

That's why I will continue to to inflict the best of my journalist/ incest survivor/ playwright/ musical theatre librettist-lyricist/gay activist/spiritual psychology/former-hippie perceptions on the whole damned nuclear mess and report what I've come up with, every week, on my show. And I'll be doing everything I can to support and promote anniversary events at Three Mile Island in the coming years, especially TMI/40 in 2019. I want to see if there's any hope that the world will finally pay attention to this nuclear meltdown that nobody died AT but did die FROM, understand the risks that the nuclear industry continues to take with life around the world, and DO something about it.

What I will do is keep digging into stories, sharing information, doing my best to keep this movement in good heart, and kicking the nuclear industry that brought us Three Mile Island in the shins… or a little bit higher.

Sometimes, I feel that all I'm doing with *Nuclear Hotseat* is narrating the rearrangement of the deck chairs on the Titanic. But then again, there are moments when I think that maybe, just maybe, I am doing some good and helping to make a difference. Maybe only a small difference. A tiny difference.

A quantum difference?

I will never know the ultimate results of my efforts, but the outcome isn't the point. I have to try. Because to not do everything I have in me and tra-la-la in self-imposed ignorance as the planetary web of life and everything it took to create it disintegrates, forever, is a crime against nature, humanity, and eternity.

How dare I, how dare we not try?

Which brings to mind only the second joke I've ever written:

How many survivors of Three Mile Island does it take to screw in a lightbulb?

All of them.

All of *us*.

And when do we start? Now? Is it NOW???

Yes. Now.

Now.

TMI/40 – A Proposal

March 28, 2019, will mark the 40th anniversary of the Three Mile Island meltdown. As I've stated before, the mainstream media only pays attention to anniversaries of disasters that end in a "5" or a "0." That means that TMI/40 in 2019 may be our last big chance to focus international attention on this long-downplayed, almost forgotten, still deadly nuclear accident. The potential exists to turn this anniversary into a national wake-up call for a population that once, in the immediate aftermath of the TMI accident, stopped the national nuclear juggernaut dead in its tracks for 30 years. Demonstrations against nuclear power plants by hundreds of thousands of people ended plans to put a thousand reactors up and down our ocean coasts, and on inland lakes and rivers. Perhaps we can inspire that again.

What kind of action will it take to create a big enough noise that the national and international media actually hear and pay attention? Visions of activists joined by community members dance in my head, and the possibilities seem endless. Note that what follows is my visioning, not yet that of any group. Still, it would be great if international activists and local community would pull together and make something extraordinary happen.

Among the possible events I envision:

- Thursday, March 28, 2019: Annual vigil at 4:00 a.m. at the gates of TMI, followed by a day of teach-ins by activists and opportunities for people who lived through the TMI accident to share their experience in privacy with others who also went through it. Meeting places could be schools, libraries, senior centers, malls – easily accessible spaces where people can drop in to safely speak their truth in an environment that will support them and respect their privacy. Maybe there could be a 12-step-type format created to guarantee safe, private sharing: Three Mile Island Anonymous, or just Nuclear Anonymous. Meetings could be held in Middletown, Goldsboro, Harrisburg, Philadelphia – anywhere a TMI survivor is willing to claim a space and stick to the format as in any 12-step environment. No recordings. All shares will be "left in the room." This will help break the isolation experienced by those who survived but have never had the opportunity to speak of it to others.

- Friday, March 29 – Town Hall meeting in Middletown that night, with presentations by various experts on nuclear safety and the health impact of radiation. Chances for residents to speak out publically, share, identify each other, and continue building community support. Livestream, record audio and video, post to social media.

- Saturday, March 30 – All day event. Main hall for plenary sessions and major speakers brought in from all over the country, if not the world. Side rooms for break-out sessions, teach-ins, Q&A, organizing. A hall with booths for information, maybe games like "pin the tail on the head of Exelon" or "Nuclear Whack-a-

Mole." Work with medical experts to prep a registry and questionnaire for those who lived through and/or believe they have been affected by the TMI accident, so we can gather the medical information before it's too late. This may be best coordinated through area doctors, medical school(s), or teaching hospital(s). Make certain all resulting data is kept in a publically accessible online database, available to all researchers, preferably for free.

- Saturday night, entertainment and a party/schmooze/ dance to work off the adrenaline.[141]
- Sunday, March 31 – Encourage area churches hold a Ceremony of Mourning. Dedicate it to those whose health and lives have been impacted by the long-term effects of radiation exposure, or who see health problems showing up in their children and grandchildren which they believe is a result of the TMI accident and radiation releases. Coordinate a time for one minute of church bells ringing and/or sirens going off as congregants hold to silence in commemoration of those who suffer, who suffered, who are dying, who died.

This is just a general outline of what might be possible. It's open for elaboration and development, coordinated with local activists and residents through a mechanism that has not yet been developed. And let me make this clear: Can "I" do this? No. But can "we" do it? If there is interest and will, absolutely.

And we must.

Whatever results, I plan to be at TMI/40. Will you?

AFTERWORD

So Whatta We Do Now, Coach?

The nuclear issue can seem so overwhelming that even if you want to get involved, it's hard to know where to start.

So let me help. What follows is a simplified trail of breadcrumbs for you to follow so you can get information without becoming overwhelmed as you join with others in working to turn around this nuclear Goliath.[142] It's not an all-inclusive list, just a few toeholds in general categories where you can find basic information and look for more. When in doubt, contact a likely group and ask about whatever it is you're interested in doing or learning. They'll be happy to help you.

GET INFORMED:
Knowledge is power: learn what you can. A good place to start is with *Nuclear Hotseat,* **www.NuclearHotseat.com**. That's where you will get weekly nuclear news as well as perspective and context to understand what each story means. There's humor, too. The show is geared to people who know nothing who want to know something, and

people who know something who want to know a little bit more. A new program posts/broadcasts every week, with the complete archive on the website or iTunes. You can sign up for a free weekly mail with a link to the episode and a summary of its contents. Be sure to check out each show's web page, where you'll find links to related information.

What follows is intended to give you a starting place for your explorations into nuclear issues so you can find a way to get involved that is appropriate for you.

BOOKS:

- *Nuclear Power is Not the Answer* and *Nuclear Madness* by Dr. Helen Caldicott. And anything else she's ever written.
- *COVER UP: What you ARE NOT SUPPOSED to KNOW ABOUT NUCLEAR POWER* by Karl Grossman. The book is hard to find in print, but it's been made available as a free download to those of you who have been reading this book at: http://www.karlgrossman.com/images/books/KarlGr ossmanCoverUpCropped.pdf
- *Full Body Burden: Growing Up in the Nuclear Shadow of Rocky Flats* by Kristen Iversen
- *No Immediate Danger* by Rosalie Bertell, PhD
- *News Zero* by Beverly Keever, on how the *New York Times* bailed on its responsibilities to report "all the news that's fit to print" in the early nuclear days and how that set us up for our current dilemma.
- *The Warning: Accident at Three Mile Island* by Mike Gray and Ira Rosen
- *Chernobyl: Consequences of the Catastrophe for People and the Environment* by Alexey Yablakov, Vassily B. Nesterenko and Alexey V. Nesterenko, edited in

English by Dr. Janette Sherman. The printed book is expensive and hard to find, but a free PDF download is available at: http://strahlentelex.de/Yablokov_Chernobyl _book.pdf,

INFORMATIONAL SITES:

On the website for the **Helen Caldicott Foundation** (www.helencaldicottfoundation.org), you will find links to her articles, books, and full videos of two post-Fukushima symposia held at the New York Academy of Medicine: The Medical and Ecological Consequences of the Fukushima Nuclear Disaster (March 11-12, 2013) and The Dynamics of Possible Nuclear Extinction (Feb. 28-March 1, 2015).

Fairewinds Energy Education (www.Fairewinds.org) is an educational hub for fact-based, undistorted nuclear energy information. Videos, articles, links, all explained with Chief Engineer Arnie Gundersen's trademarked clarity, concision, and insights.

Radiation and Public Health Project (www.radiation.com) is a nonprofit educational and scientific organization, established by scientists and physicians, dedicated to understanding the relationships between low-level nuclear radiation and public health. It studies official government health statistics and teases out the nuclear-relevant information. Epidemiologist Joseph Mangano works through this group.

Bob Alvarez, Senior Scholar at the Institute for Policy Studies, served as senior policy adviser to the Energy Department's secretary and deputy assistant secretary for National Security and the Environment, 1993-1999. If you Google his writing, you'll always find it informative and worth the read.

UNITED STATES: NATIONAL AND REGIONAL GROUPS:

Beyond Nuclear (www.BeyondNuclear.com) and **Nuclear Information and Resource Service (NIRS)** (www.NIRS.org) are excellent groups providing regular newsletters and special updates on issues as they happen. Their sites include articles, videos, podcasts, all manner of information for you to dig into on your own. Beyond Nuclear has recently expanded to cover more international issues (BeyondNuclearIntrnational.org). Sign up for email from both groups. If you have a specific question or want advice on local groups to contact, shoot them an email.

Nuclear Energy Information Service (www.NEIS.org), based in Chicago, focuses on Midwest and Great Lakes issues, including Canada's plans to build a high level radioactive waste dump within one mile of the shores of Lake Huron.

Blue Ridge Environmental Defense League (BREDL) covers nuclear issues in Virginia, North Carolina, South Carolina, Georgia, and Alabama. www.BREDL.org.

Tri Valley Cares (www.TriValleyCares.org) covers the central California coast, including Lawrence Livermore Labs and Diablo Canyon nuclear reactors, among other peace and justice issues.

There are other regional groups; do an internet search to find the ones closest and most pertinent to you.

LOCAL U.S. GROUPS:

Virtually every nuclear reactor or radioactive waste dump site has a local activist group keeping watch over it. To find a group, do an internet search under the name or your state or community and Nuclear, Radiation, the name of nuclear reactor sites, or nuclear accidents in. Wikipedia is a good place to find lists of reactors, accidents, and nuclear sites, though much of its writing about nuclear has been compromised by industry hacks and trolls rewriting history to favor their viewpoint and negate that of activists. Search for local groups on Facebook as well.

You can contact the local chapter of **Physicians for Social Responsibility** at www.PSR.org; they were originally formed by Dr. Caldicott and have a solid anti-nuclear stance as part of its DNA. Note that you do not have to be a physician to join PSR.

Sometimes a **Sierra Club** chapter will have a nuclear committee, the best being their Grassroots Network National Nuclear-Free Campaign. But note that this is not an official national stand of the Sierra Club. National leadership has been known to be quite confused about the purported "green-ness" of nuclear reactors and at least one chapter has a "gone renegade" leader who gets herself quoted in all kinds of pro-nuclear propaganda.

Greenpeace is a great, powerful force in Europe, not so much in the US, but hopefully that can change. Contact your local Greenpeace chapter and ask what they do on nuclear issues; if nothing at this time, push them to start. If they're already active, join them.

For **Three Mile Island**, as stated earlier, check out **TMI Alert** (www.TMIA.org).

CANADA:

Dr. Gordon Edwards is the head of **Canadian Coalition for Nuclear Responsibility** (www.CCNR.org) and always an excellent, easy-to-understand source.

In Ontario, the **Clean Air Alliance** (www.CleanAir Alliance.org) sends out No Nukes News every week.

For Canadian uranium mining, issues, check out Inter-Church Uranium Committee Educational Cooperative (www.facebook.com/pages/Inter-Church-Uranium-Committee-Educational-Cooperative/295038673878325?hc_location=ufi), a long-running NGO opposed to uranium mining and all that follows.

For a list of Canadian nuclear issues and groups, go to www.nuclear-heritage.net/index.php/Anti-nuclear_Movement_in_Canada.

JAPAN:

For information on the people of Japan and what has been happening to them since Fukushima, there are several good sites which translate their information into English.

From its formation at the start of the Fukushima disaster, **Tarachine Iwaki Citizens Radiation Monitoring Center** has offered services such as radiation monitoring of food. They recently opened a new clinic to test and diagnose children for radiation-related health problems that government health workers either don't or are prevented from checking. www.tarachineiwaki.org/english

3.11 Fund for Children with Thyroid Cancer similarly helps children who are not getting prompt, adequate diagnosis and treatment from the Japanese medical establishment, which is dedicated to hiding the effects of radiation on its citizens. www.311kikin.org/english

Fukushima technical information is brilliantly handled by the American-based **Simply Info** (aka **Fukuleaks**), found at www.SimplyInfo.org. It is a not-for-profit research collective that holds and manages the world's largest public archive of data on the Fukushima disaster.

For information on Hiroshima and Nagasaki, contact the **Hiroshima Peace Institute** at Hiroshima City University (http://home.hiroshima-u.ac.jp/heiwa/ipshue.html)

INTERNATIONAL:
Two excellent **news sites** are **www.Nuclear-News.net**, especially good for European news, and **www.Dianuke.org**, based in India. The new **www.BeyondNuclearInternational.org** is proving to be a good source for feature articles that go into the issues in depth, and from a human perspective.

International Physicians for the Prevention of Nuclear War (www.IPPNW.org) lives up to its name and is active around the world. Google for a chapter in your country. As with its allied Physicians for Social Responsibility, you do not have to be a physician to be a member.

Independent WHO (www.IndependentWHO.org) exposed the truth behind World Health Organization reports that minimized the impact of Chernobyl and keeps its awareness on WHO. Based in Geneva, Switzerland, Independent WHO's leader, Alison Katz, is the source of one of *Nuclear Hotseat*'s most important episodes: http://nuclearhotseat.com/2017/10/25/unwho-suppression-of-critical-chernobyl-book-devastating-stats-alison-katz-nh-331/.

Bellona Foundation (www.Bellona.org) keeps a close watch on nuclear issues in Russia, Ukraine, and all of Eastern Europe.

Chernobyl Children International (www.Chernobyl-international.com), based in Ireland and founded by Adi Roch, provides medical treatments and humanitarian aide to children suffering from radiation-based illnesses and mutations following the Chernobyl nuclear disaster.

FACEBOOK:
For all its shifting algorithm nonsense and capricious actions towards activist sites, Facebook remains a primary

way of staying aware of what's happening with nuclear issues around the world. You'll soon recognize that no matter where they show up, nuclear issues are the same the world over.

In general, when on Facebook, search out groups with the words radiation, nuclear, nukes, Fukushima, Chernobyl, or any other nuclear search term that catches your attention.

Among the dozens of groups to Like and Follow are: Coalition Against Nukes; The Rainbow Warriors; RNA International, Coalition for Nuclear Disarmament and Peace (which focuses on India and Pakistan), and so many others that it's best if you just dive in and explore for yourself.

RADIATION MONITORING:

Safecast at www.Safecast.org. Since Fukushima, this non-profit has been mapping background radiation through citizen activists and doing specific site checks if problems arise. If you want to create a local group to monitor radiation in your area, contact them. They provide workshops to teach you how to build radiation monitors from kits (cost-effective and you have a better understanding of the equipment), then they train you in their use.

The advantage of using Safecast meters is that they automatically, in real time, upload background radiation readings to an international database. All data collected by Safecast is made available for free to anyone who wants it. This is especially important if you live near a nuclear site, such as a reactor, waste dump, uranium mine, or former weapons manufacturing site, and want to be able to monitor your day-to-day risks. Good explanation from Sean Bonner on *Nuclear Hotseat* #349, February 27, 2018.

NUCLEAR WEAPONS:

The leading group fighting against nuclear weapons is the **International Campaign for the Abolition of Nuclear Weapons** (www.ICANw.org), which was awarded the 2017 Nobel Peace Prize. ICAN is the major force behind the United Nations Treaty on the Prohibition of Nuclear Weapons, which was passed by 122 nations on July 7, 2017.

As of publication, that treaty is in the ratification process; 50 countries need to officially sign on for it to become international law. For ideas on how to approach elected officials regarding the need for ratifying this treaty, which will place nuclear weapons on the same outlaw footing as landmines and chemical/biological weapons, go to the ICAN website. Their materials are clear and their actions are easy to implement.

To learn what any one of us, in any country, can do to pressure nuclear weapons producing companies, the Netherlands-based group **Don't Bank on the Bomb** (www.DontBankOnTheBomb.com) has put together a brilliant program. They maintain a complete list of companies involved in weapons manufacturing, their financials and background, as well as the financial institutions know to support them. All is available for you to study, link to, print out, and use.

The ICAN program is based on a simple, elegant concept:

- Go to your banks, pension funds, and investment companies.

- Ask if they have invested in any of the 28 companies that manufacture and/or assemble parts for nuclear weapons.
- If they have, ask that they withdraw your money from those funds or you will withdraw your money from them, and talk to everyone you know to do the same, including any investment group or pension fund to which you belong.

It's easy to do, and all necessary materials for any one of us to go to our bank are available on their website. This program has already been successful in Europe and Scandinavia, where major financial institutions and pension funds have withdrawn billions of dollars from nuclear industry investments. They did it; you can do it, too.

Nukemap, by Alex Wellerstein, allows you to visualize the impact of a nuclear weapon of any size landing any place on earth. Here's how:

- Go to: **www.nuclearsecrecy.com/nukemap**, or just google Nukemap.
- Enter a location. The default is set on Manhattan. For maximum impact, use your home city or region.
- Choose the size of the bomb. Use the drop-down menu to choose an actual bomb; always good to start with Hiroshima, because we have photos of the results of that bombing to demonstrate what would happen on the ground in your chosen location.
- Make certain you click on Casualties and Radioactive Fallout to tally that information.
- Click Detonate.

What results is a graphic representation of what a nuclear bomb would do to your immediate world. Just remember that in today's mega-bomb environment, Hiroshima can be considered a nuclear "pipsqueak." If you're putting together a PowerPoint, it's always effective to follow the bomb detonation visual with on-the-ground photographs of Hiroshima. That way, there's no confusion as to the devastation that would follow.

Also helpful in making the point about the impact of nuclear weapons is an **animation** by Japanese artist Isao Hashimoto of **every atmospheric nuclear explosion** that has ever happened. You can find it at: www.youtube.com/watch?v=LLCF7vPanrY.

Global Network Against Weapons and Nuclear Power in Space is a United States-based group with international reach. Follow their work at: www.Space4Peace.org.

Videos: The ultimate immersion in understanding what nuclear weapons will do to life and the planet can be found in the videos of Dr. Caldicott's 2015 two-day Symposium on the Dynamics of Possible Nuclear Extinction, available at: www.youtube.com/watch?v=CVud0p4aGRo or Google "Dr. Caldicott Symposium" to bring up the link.

Nuclear Age Peace Foundation is a non-profit, non-partisan international education and advocacy group. It has consultative status to the United Nations Economic and Social Council and is recognized by the UN as a Peace Messenger Organization. www.WagingPeace.org.

EASY ACTIONS:

Remember: Don't make yourself nuts! Don't try to do too much, too fast, or you risk burning out. Pick one thing you can do and do it. For example:

- Sign up for newsletters and alerts from any group that appeals to you.
- If you get a request to sign a petition, read what it's about and, if you agree, sign the petition. A second step would be to forward it to a few friends as well. Tell them what you're doing, and why.
- Donate. Every anti-nuclear group is working on a bake sale budget. Anything you can send will help. Don't assume your donation is too small to make a difference. *Nuclear Hotseat* has a special green Donate Now button on the website to easily set up a $5/month recurring donation, and it's those small, regular donations that have kept the show running.
- Online Marketing. If you have internet marketing experience, there's not a single anti-nuclear group that doesn't need your advice and help. Volunteer to guide them into a more savvy online presence.
- If you're ready to step up your game, make a comment to the Nuclear Regulatory Commission on an issue under their consideration. You'll get notified of these possibilities through email from the groups you join, which usually include suggested talking points. Know that even if you're not an "expert," you have an opinion that's worth hearing – and the NRC wants to be able to count on you not voicing it. Let's surprise them, shall we?

PERSONAL SUGGESTIONS:

When you first begin your own nuclear explorations, pace yourself. You don't have to read/listen/do it all immediately. Learn about one issue that piques your interest. Pick one action. Do it and digest it. Repeat. It helps to have others to whom you can talk this over, because you can bet this topic will not be welcomed as light conversation around the Thanksgiving table. Being part of a larger anti-nuclear group can provide you with others who will be able to listen to you and talk about it without requiring footnotes.

If there is no nuclear-concerned group in your area, form one! It doesn't have to be big and elaborate; *Nuclear Hotseat* started as a conference call with two people on it and absolutely no idea where it was heading. Put a post up on Facebook, Twitter, an announcement in your neighborhood newspaper, Pennysaver, or on NextDoor.com. Find just one other person ("Where two or more are gathered…") and – TA DA! – you're a group. Sit down together and talk about your concerns. Get your local library involved. (I LOVE libraries and librarians; their support to my work has been deeply heartening.)

Libraries can provide you with meeting space and places to post flyers for, say, an anti-nuclear book club. Pick a book, read it together, discuss.

Connect with any of the established groups in your state or a national group for support. Share fears. Brainstorm actions. Take nuclear issues out from the shadows where we've been taught to hide them and find one upon which you wish to shed light. Then go light the candles, turn on your flashlights, focus the klieg lights, and let your immediate world know.

And don't burn out! When I started *Nuclear Hotseat* in 2011, I knew very little about nuclear issues beyond what I'd learned in the 1950's and for a brief time after TMI. Sometimes my learning curve on the show was so steep, it felt vertical. That's when I'd take time out, go to nature, and remind myself of why I do this work in the first place.

Pace yourself. Play the long game. Remember: plutonium, with its half-life of 24,000 years, will still be around and radioactive when you're ready to move back into action...

As will *Nuclear Hotseat*.

ACKNOWLEDGEMENTS

As a newbie to nuclear activism since March 11 of 2011, I hold enormous respect and gratitude for all the activists, scientists, engineers, doctors, and creative thinkers who have shared information through publishing, broadcasting, online media, and personal connection. An all-inclusive list would take another full book, but here are a few who made the deepest impact upon me, with my apologies for any omissions.

First and foremost, Dr. Helen Caldicott. I have often referred to her as "The Goddess Athena" for her warrior spirit, caring heart, brilliant intellect, and seemingly inexhaustible supply of energy. She's been out there on the nuclear issue consistently for more than 40 years, carrying the torch and leading the way, even if at times it seemed that no one was following. I, and we, owe her an immeasurable debt of gratitude.

National activist leaders quickly stepped to the fore with reliable information early on when so much was hidden by hysteria or suppression. These included Michael Mariotte and Mary Olson of NIRS, Kevin Kamps and Cindy Folkers of Beyond Nuclear. Each of these women and men helped orient me to the awfulness of the Fukushima news as I moved from shock and depression into action. Nuclear engineer and former industry insider Arnie Gundersen of Fairewinds Energy Education emerged as our own "Mr. Wizard," whose presence in YouTube videos explained the horrors of Fukushima calmly, accurately, and in language even the uninitiated (such as myself) could follow. He and Maggie Gundersen operate Fairewinds Energy Education, where he continues to be a rock-solid source for reliable information on nuclear from both the engineering and the human perspective.

Regular sources who have provided features for *Nuclear Hotseat* include: Shaun McGee (nee: Arclight) and Hervé Courtois of Nuclear-News.net; ferocious fireball Mimi German of No Nuke NW; Erica Gray of the Nuclear Free Campaign of the Sierra Club; Dave Parrish of Operation SAVE the Earth; and everyone who sends me tips, leads, links, and story suggestions.

I've come to know and love the tenacious California activists for their intelligence, ferocity of spirit, and relentless action on behalf of all who live in the shadow of San Onofre, Diablo Canyon, and the Santa Susana Field Laboratory. Specifically, I salute Donna Gilmore of SanOnofreSafety.org, Gary and Laurie Headrick of San Clemente Green, Gene Stone of Residents Organized for a Safe Environment, and nuclear tech interpreter extraordinaire Ace Hoffman of the DAB Safety Team. The northern California activists who fight Diablo Canyon, Lawrence Livermore Labs, and keep a close eye on the California Public Utilities Commission include but are not limited to: Jane Swanson of San Luis Obispo Mothers for Peace and Marylia Kelley of Tri-Valley CARES, award-winning documentarians Mary Beth Brangan and Jim Brangan of Ecological Options Network (EON3.net), ombudsman Roger Herried, and Kimberly Roberson of Fukushima Fallout Awareness Network, who from the first has kept track of radiation contamination of the food chain. Kimberly, a Certified Nutrition Educator, became my partner on a six-audio series we recorded on protection from radiation: *Radiation Awareness Protection Talk (RAPT)*.

A special acknowledgement to Priscilla Star, founder of the Coalition Against Nukes (CAN), who has helped me with her personal passion, unflinching support, and ginormous heart. And a bow of respect to ace investigative journalist and nuclear *éminence grise* Karl Grossman for his encouragement to finish this book. Karl, I made it. Thanks.

I don't know what I would have done to round out this book if I hadn't gotten to Three Mile Island for the 39th anniversary and panel discussion. Deep gratitude to Beverly Findlay-Kaneko, Yuji Kaneko, and Jim Torson for giving me the boost I needed in the form that I needed at the time that I needed it most.

Further gratitude to my Facebook friends and information sources around the world who let me know what nuclear looks like from their perspectives: Kevin Hester of New Zealand for his decades of climate change activism and cheeky doomer humor; Kumar Sundaram for his relentless presentation of India's nuclear truth; Dennis Riches of Japan; Marius Paul and Candyce Paul of the Denesulineh Indigenous Nation, Popular/Aspen Tree Home Human Beings, People of the Headwaters, Caribou-Eater dialect presently based in (settler parlance) Northern Saskatchewan. Any names I may have left off, know it's not from lack of admiration for who you are and what you do.

A commemoration for the ones we've lost since I joined this powerful movement: Barbara George of Women's Energy Matters, whose loving presence and ferocious activism here in California are deeply missed; Michael Mariotte, Executive Director of Nuclear Information and Resource Service (NIRS), who opened the door for me and remained a valuable contact; Dr. Stephen Wing, the epidemiologist who cracked the lie that "nobody died at

Three Mile Island;" and the great Dr. Alexey Yablakov, grandfather of Russian environmentalism and former advisor to Mikhail Gorbachev, who gathered medical and research reports on Chernobyl from non-English-speaking countries and compiled them into the book, *Chernobyl: Consequences of the Catastrophe for People and the Environment.*

My gratitude to all the *Nuclear Hotseat* interviewees and correspondents in the U.S., Canada, Japan, India, Australia, New Zealand, Brazil, Austria, Switzerland, Germany, France, the UK, South Africa, and anywhere else you may be. You are, each of you, making a difference in the world through your willingness to be aware and take action. May the results we seek come soon enough.

Thanks for the boost and support in getting *Nuclear Hotseat* out into the world by syndicators Jules Stan and Patrick Wilson, along with the Pacifica Audioport crew Otis Maclay and Ursula Ruedenberg. Other outlets are "getting with the program" and I expect the list of stations and syndicators to grow. For in-person presentations, thanks to librarians Ania Bloch and Mark Totten, and the staff of TEDxPasadena.

When the dark night of the writing soul comes, it's important to have writerly support such as I received from my gentle editor, Carol Woodliff. And how did I ever survive without the manic email support of dark fantasy/horror writer (in her second language, no less!) Ksenia Anske, who relentlessly bullied me in the nicest way possible into once again loving the writing process? My heartfelt gratitude to both of these creative forces of nature.

Here's to my Mastermind partner/tech savior/marketing guru Richard Villasana. The internet would never have heard of me without your hands-on help and guidance, offered with patience and kindness straight from your heart. You're one of the ultimate good guys. Other tech and marketing thanks to my business mentors: June Davidson, Eric Lofholm, Arvee Robinson, and Rick Cooper. And many thanks to my spiritual mentors, Dr. Ron Hulnick and Dr. Mary Hulnick of the University of Santa Monica.

On the personal front, my gratitude for the healing hearts of the late Sharon Tobin, the late Dr. Marjorie Braude, Larry Lincoln, Anne Lincoln, Shannon Steck, Sharon Burnett, and the compassionate crew at Safe Harbors.

Personal friends have helped me through many years, eras, and past lives that were lived within this body: Dr. Diane Berrier Sandler, both friend and healer, who among her many generosities loaned me office space to retreat and get writing of the first draft done; Robin Rader, who helped solve the mystery of my title and is my favorite Scrabble™ partner; Joyce Joyce Mason, Suzanne Fox, Hermione Weiss, Prof. James "Max" Saslow, Joseph K. Adams, the Mt. Washington Goddesses, and energy healer extraordinaire as well as dear friend Barbara Robins.

Immeasurable good in my life would not have been possible without the love and support of my dear friend Joan Hotchkis. A special salute to you, my dear.

Finally, my heart goes out to Rachel and Alan. I did it, I do it, for you.

Love and Light, Namaste, Masi Cho, Mitaquioyasin, Shalom, Salaam, Peace – and No Nukes,

Libbe HaLevy
July 16, 2018

ABOUT THE AUTHOR

Libbe HaLevy (lee-BEE ha-LAY-vee) is the producer and host of *Hotseat*, a weekly program about nuclear issues... "from a different perspective." In weekly production since June, 2011, the podcast is downloaded in 123 countries, available at NuclearHotseat.com and on iTunes, and syndicated for a growing number of broadcast stations through Pacifica's Audioport network.

Libbe is the co-creator of *Radiation Awareness Protection Talk*, or *RAPT*, a six-audio series on best possible practices to protect against nuclear radiation. A book and ebook are in the works.

Her articles have appeared in the *LA Times, Boston Globe, Village Voice*, and *LA Weekly*, and she's been a columnist for seven different publications. She has served as a Writing, Business and Recovery coach for Peak Potentials, American Seminar Leaders Association, and a private clientele which includes stage and screen star Julie Andrews (for whom she facilitated a business retreat), children's literacy expert Emma Walton Hamilton, and Dr. Michael Rabinoff, a first-time writer whose book has been endorsed by the Dalai Lama.

An award-winning playwright and librettist, Libbe's musical *Now, Voyager*, based on the same source material as the beloved Bette Davis movie, was optioned for Broadway, featured at the ASCAP/Disney Musical Theatre, was winner of the Spirit of Moondance Award at the Moondance International Film Festival, and recipient of the Anna Sosenko Trust Grant.

Her play *SHATTERED SECRETS*, a Moondance finalist,

ran 2-1/2 years in Santa Monica and has been produced internationally. *SECRETS,* a version of *SHATTERED SECRETS* incorporating music and choreographic movement, was directed by Tony™ Award-winner Grover Dale and produced by original *A Chorus Line* member Michel Stuart. Her other plays include the Carolyn Cycle, which in addition to *SHATTERED SECRETS* consists of *Pearls that Coalesce, Sexual Sushi,* and the award-winning *Thanksgiving.*

HaLevy recently completed a two-character two-act tour-de-force play, *Marilyn: The Final Session,* about Marilyn Monroe and a feminist therapist meeting in Purgatory to work through issues of femininity, abuse, and power. It is not a musical. Her one-woman shows include *Confessions of a Peri-Menopausal Novice Backpacker* and *Hair, Radiation, Revolution.*

HaLevy co-founded Broadway on Sunset (BOS), a Los Angeles-based musical theatre development organization, and has taught musical theatre libretto writing at The Songwriters Guild of America, the National Academy of Songwriters, and Highways Performance Space.

She holds a Masters of Spiritual Psychology from the University of Santa Monica and a BA in Radio-TV Communications from the University of Illinois.

To book Libbe HaLevy as a broadcast or podcast guest, keynote speaker, or workshop/seminar leader, send an email to:

YesIGlowintheDark@gmail.com

ENDNOTES

Chapter 1

[1] Interestingly, Godzilla was created for the 1954 movie of that name by director Ishiro Honda, who made it clear in an interview that the monster *Gojira* (Godzilla) was designed to embody the characteristics of a living atomic bomb. Interestingly, Honda was born in Yamagata Prefecture, which is only 35 miles from Fukushima.
http://motherboard.vice.com/blog/godzilla-is-our-never-ending-nuclear-nightmare

[2] Now known as the Society of Professional Journalists

[3] Boston gay groups benefitted from a unique challenge faced by local media. Every winter, blizzards regularly shut down Logan Airport, cancelling flights and preventing guests from being able to fulfill their bookings. I positioned myself as the emergency last-minute go-to provider of interesting local guests. Many's the time I got a frantic call from producers with less than 24 –hours notice to airtime and provided them with reps from groups such as Dykes and Tykes (lesbian mothers) or the Homophile Community Health Service.

[4] This was before the words "Lesbian," "Bisexual" and "Transsexual" were added to its name.

[5] Much more is involved, but that's the material for another book. The *Welby* protest and my involvement in it is the subject of an upcoming documentary by filmmaker Duane Andersen.

[6] My birth name, still in force in those days, was Loretta Lotman. I changed it in 1985 to signify a major shift in consciousness and the healing work I was doing.

Chapter 2

[7] "Jeanne" and "Jim" are both pseudonyms, as over the years we lost touch and I have been unable to locate them for permission to use their real names.

[8] Video of the Walter Cronkite/CBS Special Report on Three Mile Island can be found here:
https://www.YouTube.com/watch?v=QVu92rk4M0Q

[9] More than 30 years later, I learned the devices didn't work because the radiation releases far exceeded anything the equipment had been built to withstand. In other words, the monitors were fried by radiation levels beyond anything the government wanted us to know. More on Three Mile Island radiation releases and the ignored times for evacuation here:
http://www.fairewinds.com/content/three-myths-three-mile-island-accident

Chapter 3

[10] I've not a clue what they were or where they are.

[11] It took me approximately 16 years before I had the courage to view *The China Syndrome*. Much as I'd feared, I had a visceral fear response and walked out of the theater stunned. It took several weeks and a lot of chocolate to pull myself back to a semblance of being together.

Chapter 5

[12] Of small comfort was the discovery that the musical scene I'd sent to Theodore Chapin, then head of the Musical Theatre Lab in New York, wound up on that group's bulletin board for all to read. I never learned if the posting was meant as appreciative or ironic.

[13] The jury was hung with respect to the Ray Buckey verdict on 13 of the 52 counts against him. District Attorney Reiner retried Ray Buckey on eight counts involving three girls. The jury was hung on all counts, and D. A. Ira Reiner decided not to ask for a third trial of Ray Buckey. [14] A second trial on unresolved charges ended in a hung jury on all counts.

Chapter 6

[15] Abby Mann, who produced *Judgment at Nuremburg* and *Kojak*, came on board as media consultant to the owners of that preschool.

[16] The show has lain fallow ever since. If you're interested, email me at:
YesIGlowIntheDark@gmail.com.

[17] The play had its influence: for a while, it seemed that every TV movie had either the word "shattered" or "secret" in the title.

Chapter 7

[18] Unfortunately, that policy began collapsing as of 2017, when for the first time a US naval vessel was allowed into NZ waters. It took part in the Royal New Zealand Navy's hosting of a 15-nation International Naval Review to mark the 75th anniversary of the country's existence. It's a safe bet that since this line has been crossed, it will not be the last time that one or more U.S. nuclear-powered if not nuke-carrying ships or planes will be allowed into New Zealand waters and/or airspace.

[19] Yes, I know a lot of you are vegetarians, but some people still eat meat. Deal with it. We have more important things to squabble about.

[20] I highly recommend this tactic for everyone, even men and post-menopausal women. Just ask for the same level of protection as would be given a pregnant woman.

[21] Not my *only* job, but as producer, I was the one she trusted with that tricky, intimate bit of staging.

Chapter 8

[22] The truth is that after exposure to radiation, the cancer clock never stops running.

[23] To be honest, I was never big on visiting doctors and diagnostic tests. I didn't even acknowledge that my growing exhaustion might be because of a medical condition; I just assumed this was the way it was, growing older.

[24] Learn more about the Cellular Yoga™ work of Dr. Diane Sandler, Lac CST-D at: www.DianeSandler.com.

[25] The basic premise of Spiritual Psychology is that we don't look at ourselves as human beings having a spiritual experience; we are divine beings having a human experirnce, and the challenges we face are the curriculum we signed up for in "Earth school" to resolve our karmic issues. It truly is "a different perspective."

[26] Hats off to composer Stormy Sachs and lyricist Robert Battan.

[27] Ironically, in setting up our first work session, composer Jay Gruska and I exchanged email on March 11, 2011 – the same day that the Fukushima nuclear disaster began.

Chapter 9

[28] Actually, the devastation at Fukushima Daiichi began with the earthquake, which ruptured steam and water pipes. The disaster has been framed as having been caused by the tsunami to make the event of such an accident happening again seem remote, but the initial damage was done by the quake and then made worse by the tsunami.

29 The numbers remain "untold," as an accurate measurement of the radiation released and continuing to be released from Fukushima has never been made… or if it has, the public has not been given access to the numbers. More recent estimates put the amount of radiation released as the equivalent of 14,000 Hiroshima bombs.

30 The New York Times labeled them "The Fukushima 50" in an article published on March 15, 2011:
www.nytimes.com/**2011**/03/16/world/asia/16workers.html

31 When TEPCO officials in Tokyo learned that ocean water was being sprayed onto the reactors, they angrily ordered plant manager Masao Yoshida to stop flooding the site because salt water would damage the equipment. If Yoshida had not followed his conscience, defied his bosses, and continued to pour water onto the site, it is entirely possible that Japan and much of the Northern Hemisphere by now would have become lethal to life.

32 TEPCO did not admit that the reactors had gone into meltdown until two months after the earthquake and tsunami. Only in February, 2016 – almost five years later – did they admit that they should have made the announcement earlier, and in June of 2016 they finally issued an apology for their delay. Right – like that did any good.
http://www.bbc.com/news/world-asia-35650625

33 Based on new information only accessed in early 2018, one week after the Fukushima Daiichi nuclear meltdowns began, TEPCO executives read the reactor's operational manual and decided the amount of water Yoshida was having poured onto the reactors was excessive. They gave the order to decrease the amount of water being poured on the reactors to keep them cool. Under duress, plant manager Masao Yoshida complied. Within 24 hours, the reactors heated up so dangerously that three additional radiation plumes were released, at which point Yoshida again increased the water supply and cooled them down. Nancy Foust of SimplyInfo.org explains these new findings on Nuclear Hotseat #363, June 5, 2018 - http://nuclearhotseat.com/2018/06/06/tepco-nuclear-error-fukushima-terror-nancy-foust-on-newly-discovered-2011-fukushima-radiation-releases

34 A billion dollar class action lawsuit has been filed on behalf of the sailors, who are being represented by former senator and US Vice Presidential candidate John Edwards, along with original attorneys Charles Bonner and Paul C. Garner. As of this writing, the wrangling continues as to whether the case should be tried in the US or Japan.

35 Despite the magnitude of three nuclear reactors in meltdown, at least one major explosion that spewed nuclear fuel into the jet stream and at least a mile away on the ground, and no possibility of containment, the New York Times and all other media have resisted calling Fukushima "the *worst* nuclear accident," even though by any metrics chosen, it is. Only in April, 2018, were announcements finally made that, yes, Fukushima is now officially the worst nuclear power disaster in history: https://www.counterpunch.org/2018/04/27/move-over-chernobyl-fukushima-is-now-officially-the-worst-nuclear-power-disaster-in-history/

36 The product I found was Natural Cellular Defense 2, or NCD2, by Waiora. It can only be bought through a distributor and I am one – not because I have a deep craving to shill for any MLM product, but because it's the best quality zeolite I have found and this is the only way to get it. More information at: http://nuclearhotseat.com/store/

37 Two years later, I collaborated with Kimberly Roberson, a Certified Nutrition Educator and founder of the Fukushima Fallout Awareness network to record a six-audio series which covers the best possible practices for self-protection from radiation. To learn more, check out Radiation Awareness Protection Talk (RAPT) at: www.RAPTawareness.com.

38 This according to the gold standard BEIR VII report of the National Academy of Science.

Chapter 11

39 http://www.enviroreporter.com/2012/08/no-place-to-hide-fukushima-fallout-findings-widespread/all/1

40 Thank you, Tim Smith!

41 I'll always feel sheepish towards the very busy Dan Hirsch of Committee to Bridge the Gap for having imposed upon his tolerance in this way.

42 Apparently that conversation took place before we recorded or I edited it out, because it's no longer on the recording.

43 This quote is taken from the film about Murrow, "Good Night and Good Luck." I'm still tracking down the source material, but I don't believe producers Grant Henslov and George Clooney would make up such an important line of dialog.

44 Introduced in 1949, The Fairness Doctrine was a policy that required the holders of broadcast licenses to present controversial issues of public importance and to do so in a manner that was—in the FCC's view—honest, equitable, and balanced. The FCC eliminated the policy in 1987

and removed the rule that implemented the policy from the *Federal Register* in August 2011.

[45] In the beginning, I avoided most stories about nuclear weapons because they dealt with what seemed to be an entirely different set of issues than reactors. However, I've learned that the split between weapons and reactor issues are an illusion, an artificial split encouraged by the nuclear industry. With that in mind, I'm covering more bomb-related issues.

[46] As of 2017, Nuclear Hotseat was picked up for syndication to community broadcast radio stations through the Pacifica Audioport network. It's now carried by a growing roster of broadcast stations.

Chapter 12

[47] Boiling Water Reactor, Physicians for Social Responsibility, International Atomic Energy Agency, San Onofre Nuclear Generating Station, Nuclear Information and Resource Service.

[48] When one factors in the carbon toll taken by nuclear for uranium mining, transport, refinement, transport of refined ore to be turned into weapons or fuel rods, shipment to nuclear reactors, then storage of "spent fuel" that require some form of cooling, containment and security for tens of thousands of years, as well as construction materials for nuclear reactors ,their transport, and then decommissioning, the carbon footprint of nuclear is enormous and never-ending. For more information, see: http://www.nirs.org/factsheets/nuclearenergyisdirtyenergy.pdf and http://www.washingtonsblog.com/2013/04/nuclear-is-not-a-low-carbon-source-of-energy.html

[49] Indeed, I joined the Society of Professional Journalists in 2015, only to leave after a frustrating year in which not only was my work not taken seriously, one of my local chapter's honchos dismissed me to my face as a "mere podcaster."

[50] Since the San Onofre reactor permanent shut down was announced in June, 2013, the sirens have been removed – meaning if there is an accident with the dry cask radioactive fuel storage or the "spent" fuel pool, there is no way to warn the local community.

[51] www.nuclearsavage.com - A documentary about the bombing of the Marshall Islands and the aftermath. The film was commissioned by the PBS *Frontline* series but never aired by them.

[52] I wrote the jingle; vocals and arrangement by Merilee Weber, accompaniment by John Barnard, recorded at Winslow Court Studios in Hollywood.

[53] Access nine years worth of daily NRC Event Notification Reports here: https://www.nrc.gov/reading-rm/doc-collections/event-status/event

54 Would that newspapers printed a summary of these NRC reported reactor events the way community newspapers publish a weekly police blotter roundup. Faced with the weekly truth of the frequency and severity of nuclear problems, I believe public opinion would change about the advisability of using nuclear reactors.

55 NRC Event Report of January 12, 2013.

56 Nuclear Hotseat #86, February 6, 2013: http://nuclearhotseat.com/2013/02/26/89-world-premiere-of-filmmaker-christopher-nolands-3-11-surviving-japan/

57 Catch the film here: https://www.youtube.com/watch?v=IKqXu-5jw60

58 Incredibly, duck-and-cover is once again being touted by "experts" as the best possible response to a nuclear incident, and by a member of the Science and Security Board of the Bulletin of the Atomic Scientists: https://www.washingtonpost.com/news/politics/wp/2017/12/14/how-to-prepare-for-a-nuclear-attack/?utm_term=.16d190126096&wpisrc=nl_rainbow&wpmm=1

59 Nuclear reactors are the most expensive, dangerous method ever designed to boil water to create steam to turn generators to create electricity – that's right, split the atom to make steam.

60 Regulatory capture is a form of government failure which occurs when a regulatory agency, created to act in the public interest, instead advances the commercial or political concerns of special interest groups that dominate the industry or sector it is charged with regulating.

61https://www.capecod.com/newscenter/nrc-to-commissioners-pilgrim-making-progress-but-concerns-remain/

62 http://www.capecodtimes.com/news/20161206/nrc-email-pilgrim-plant-overwhelmed

63 Apparently, an NRC or Entergy PR employee with the first name Diane and a last name that started with a "T" was right next to Cape Downwinder Diane Turco's information in the smartphone contact list of the leader of a NRC inspection team. Many's the slip between the eye and the thumb, and the "wrong" Diane (from the NRC's and Entergy's perspective) got the email.

64 It's roughly equivalent to the curies of Cesium-137 release from the 1986 Chernobyl disaster. Based on the Bob Alvarez report posted at SanOnofreSafety.org: https://sanonofresafety.files.wordpress.com/2018/06/songs_spent_fuel_final-alvarez.pdf

65 Never ask that question when dealing with nuclear. Never.

66 240,000 years, remember?

67https://www.nrc.gov/reactors/operating/ops-experience/reactor-vessel-integrity.html
68 www.nrc.gov/reactors/operating/licensing/renewal/overview.html
www.nbcnews.com/id/43556350/ns/us_news-environment/t/how-long-can-nuclear-reactors-last-us-industry-extend-spans/#.Wqf47jlG0b1

Chapter 13
69 Check out the studies done by researcher Dr. Ian Fairlie at www.IanFairlie.org and epidemiologist Joseph Mangano of Radiation and Public Health Project at www.radiation.org. After that, keep digging. The information's there if you look for it.
70 And even then, we're not out of the woods, as the Nuclear Decay Chain turns radioactive isotopes into other radioactive isotopes with half-lives all their own. From uranium dug out of the ground into completely inert lead takes 1.5 BILLION years. Essentially, we're talking about a source of life-threatening contamination that remains dangerous forever.
71 Karl Grossman generously makes an updated edition of *COVER UP: What you ARE NOT SUPPOSED to KNOW ABOUT NUCLEAR POWER* available in a free pdf that you can download at: http://www.karlgrossman.com/images/books/KarlGrossmanCoverUpCro pped.pdf
72 *COVER UP*, ibid.
73 My thanks to Dr. Gordon Edwards of the Canadian Coalition for Nuclear Responsibility for the Midas analogy.
74 That presupposes humanity has the knowledge, will, and resources to build another containment structure when it's needed. If we've destroyed civilization back to the stone age, as climate change activists warn will happen, the ability to encapsulate radioactive waste on such a massive scale will be lost forever, meaning the Chernobyl structure will decay until it cracks and leaks, and then Earth will have to deal with Chernobyl all over again. Nuclear is truly "the gift that keeps on giving."
75 I know of one man with questionable creds that have never been seriously questioned, who hired a press rep to get him on radio programs. He then claimed his presence on the radio programs proved his legitimacy as an "expert."
76http://dels.nas.edu/resources/static-assets/materials-based-on-reports/reports-in-brief/beir_vii_final.pdf This is a summary of BEIR VII sponsored by the U.S. Department of Defense, U.S. Department of Energy, U.S. Nuclear Regulatory Commission, U.S. Environmental Protection Agency, and U.S. Department of Homeland Security. For the full BEIR VII

report, contact: BEIR VII: Health Risks from Exposure to Low Levels of Ionizing Radiation is available from the National Academies Press, 500 Fifth Street, NW, Washington, DC 20001; 800-624-6242; www.nap.edu

[77] If you want to get a jump on the upcoming nuclear spin-speak words after *immediate* and *imminent* have exhausted their power to trick us, here's a link to an online thesaurus that will show you the rest of the industry's PR-approved word list:

www.thesaurus.com/browse/immediate.

[78] The word "specks" appeared regularly in Hanford articles originating from the Tri-City Herald, the newspaper in the company town closest to Hanford. I emailed a request for a definition of the imprecise term "specks" in light of the BEIR VII report. They wrote, "The use of the word "specks" was not intended to be a comment on the hazards of the material, [just a] visual reference." The term has since disappeared from the articles on Hanford's plutonium contamination problem. Coincidence?

[79] San Onofre played its own semantic tricks, as the full name – San Onofre Nuclear Generating Station – became the acronym "SONGS." So opposing "SONGS" made it subliminally sound like activists hated music. And it had to be intentional: no other nuclear facility in the country is referred to as a "nuclear generating station."

[80] San Onofre owner/operator Southern California Edison claims it was "economics" that shut down San Onofre. But they don't admit that they tried to game the steam generator design to squeeze more electricity out of it by authorizing an unapproved design change that took out a large number of safety features. When steam generator pipes leaked radiation, it led to an emergency shutdown. Examination by the NRC revealed wear and damage to the fuel rods associated with 30 years of operation – but the problems showed up after only 11 months. The nuclear reactors at San Onofre were never turned on again. Details recounted on Nuclear Hotseat #364 - http://nuclearhotseat.com/2018/06/13/san-onofre-5-years-shutdown-problems-continue-charles-langley-nina-babiarz-nh-364/

[81] The decommissioning process at San Onofre is its own can of worms, most notably what to do with 890,000 spent fuel rods, comprising 1,800 tons of highly radioactive, plutonium-containing radwaste that it generated. Plans have already moved forward to store this deadly material in 5/8"thick steel "tin can" thin canisters on-site, only 125 feet from the Pacific ocean, within 50 miles of almost 8-1/2 million people. To understand how bad this is, consider that each "thin" canister contains a Chernobyl's-worth of radioactivity. One failure in one can, and we can kiss southern California goodbye.

http://www.latimes.com/local/california/la-me-stranded-nuclear-waste-20170702-htmlstory.html

[82] This is how India got the atom bomb, with Plutonium 239 extracted from an "Atoms for Peace" nuclear reactor the U.S. gave them. Karl Grossman, *COVER UP: What you ARE NOT SUPPOSED to KNOW ABOUT NUCLEAR POWER*, Page 13.

[83] For a while, I engaged in a running correspondence with the New York Times Tokyo Bureau Chief, Martin Fackler, about changing their wording. He never did, but that may just have reflected policy set by others who are higher up at the Gray Lady.

[84] https://emergency.cdc.gov/radiation/measurement.asp

[85] e.g, the Atomic Energy Commission turned itself into the Nuclear Regulatory Commission

[86]https://www.nrc.gov/about-nrc/emerg-preparedness/about-emerg-preparedness/emerg-classification.html
This is the source for all quotes on NRC Event Classifications in this section.

[87] Emphasis added.

[88] Emphasis added.

[89] https://public-blog.nrc-gateway.gov/2012/07/03/how-the-nrc-is-funded-following-the-money/

[90] ibid

[91] International manipulations would require an entire other chapter, if not another book.

[92] Former Commissioner Gregory Jaczko (2005-2012) was NRC Chair during Fukushima. In its wake, he convened hearings that led to mandated safety upgrades in US reactors – something that threatened to cost a lot of money at those facilities that couldn't wriggle out of it. After he left the NRC, Jaczko proved unemployable within the nuclear industry. He's seen as a cautionary tale. Learn more in Ivy Meeropol's film, *Indian Point*. http://indianpointfilm.com

[93] Except in the bottom line of the companies contracted to do the work.

[94] Nuclear Hotseat #338 with Arnie Gundersen's full presentation here: http://ow.ly/Rcso30hcZwo

[95] Information on William Lawrence, the *New York Times*' complicity in the radiation cover-up, and Wilfred Burchett's reporting for the London *Daily Express* is sourced from *News Zero: The New York Times and the Bomb* by Beverly Ann Deepe Keever.

[96] I believe William Lawrence's Pulitzer should be withdrawn.

[97] Full text of Burchett's article here:

https://assets.cambridge.org/97805217/18264/excerpt/9780521718264_excerpt.pdf

[98] Burchett's work was further tarred by his being known as a Communist, a factoid that makes absolutely no difference to his reporting quality or accuracy, but sufficient to discount him as a source. To this day, the first sentence of virtually every entry about the man online includes that C-word.

[99] To help in your activist work, make a record of the names of every media person you talk with. Follow up with an email thanking them for their openness. Send tips and comments on other stories. Develop a relationship.

[100] http://nuclearhotseat.com/2018/03/27/three-mile-island-yes-people-died-are-dying-tmi-39th-anniversary-special-nh-353/

[101] See: back cover. I was lucky; he had a good eye.

[102] Indeed, none of the people I spoke with had heard a word about the panel discussion for the 39th anniversary.

[103] One of those shots appears on the back cover of this book.

Chapter 15

[104] Also on the panel were reporters Michelle LeFever and David Sollenberger, who added their experiences to the event but whose stories did not impact me personally.

[105] Frank Goldstein did share one good thing that came out of Three Mile Island – the formation of FEMA, the Federal Emergency Management Agency. No such agency existed until TMI proved the need.

[106] Heidi is shooting and editing a film series on environmental disasters, *Accidents Can Happen*, and Three Mile Island is definitely one of her subjects.

[107] Retraumatization, if not recontamination. I know not how radioactive the soil, water and atmosphere are in that area. To me, it makes no difference; it's all emotionally and spiritually toxic.

Chapter 16

[108] http://nuclearhotseat.com/2018/04/11/three-mile-island-nuclear-meltdown-at-39-wtf-actually-happened-to-us-nh-355/

[109] http://www.fairewinds.com/content/three-myths-three-mile-island-accident

[110] Excellent blow-by-blow description of what happened at TMI is in Mike Gray and Ira Rosen's book, *The Warning: Accident at Three Mile Island* - https://www.amazon.com/Warning-Accident-Island-Nuclear-Terror/dp/0393324699

[111] This audio is part of the annual *Nuclear Hotseat* Three Mile Island Special, most recently as part of Episode #353, March 27, 2018: http://nuclearhotseat.com/2018/03/27/three-mile-island-yes-people-died-are-dying-tmi-39th-anniversary-special-nh-353/

[112] *The Warning*, ibid this entire section

[113] Mary Stamos interview on *Nuclear Hotseat* #353: http://nuclearhotseat.com/2018/03/27/three-mile-island-yes-people-died-are-dying-tmi-39th-anniversary-special-nh-353/

[114] http://tmia.com/node/1167

[115] https://news.psu.edu/story/325718/2014/09/10/research/thyroid-cancer-rates-pennsylvania-rising-faster-rest-country

[116] Another spin-speak. A "partial" meltdown is like being "a little bit pregnant." It either melted down or it didn't – and it did.

[117] Wing, S., Richardson, D., Crawford-Brown D. 1997 "A Reevaluation of Cancer Incidence near the Three Mile Island Nuclear Plant: The Collision of Evidence and Assumptions." *Environmental Health Perspectives* 106:52-57

[118] https://www.nirs.org/wp-content/uploads/reactorwatch/accidents/tmihealthchronology.pdf

[119] http://www.beyondnuclear.org/tmi-truth/ This is a basic orientation to Three Mile Island. Under the heading, "No One Died at TMI: The biggest lie," click on Full Backgrounder to get more information on health compromises.

[120] https://www.amazon.com/Nuclear-Power-Answer-Helen-Caldicott/dp/1595580670?SubscriptionId=AKIAILSHYYTFIVPWUY6Q&tag=duckduckgo-ffsb-20&linkCode=xm2&camp=2025&creative=165953&creativeASIN=1595580670

[121] https://www.fairewinds.org/nuclear-energy-education//three-mile-island-38th-anniversary-presentation?rq=three%20mile%20island

[122] http://journals.sagepub.com/doi/pdf/10.2968/060005010

[123] https://www.ianfairlie.org/news/childhood-leukemias-near-nuclear-power-stations-new-article/

[124] https://www.facebook.com/groups/875561992580399/?ref=br_rs Other groups have similar names, but this is the one I find best.

[125] www.TMIA.com

[126] http://tmia.com/node/1167

[127] Information on so-called "thin casks" from San Onofre Safety: www.SanOnofreSafety.org

[128] http://www.businessinsider.com/photos-of-survival-condo-project-

luxury-doomsday-shelter-2017-4#the-bunker-plans-to-feed-homeowners-
for-years-to-come-it-raises-tilapia-in-fish-tanks-and-vegetables-under-
grow-lamps-a-miniature-grocery-store-is-also-in-the-works-13
[129]https://www.medicalnewstoday.com/articles/288916.php,
http://www.cancerresearchuk.org/about-us/cancer-news/press-
release/2015-02-04-1-in-2-people-in-the-uk-will-get-cancer
[130]https://www.ianfairlie.org/news/childhood-leukemias-near-nuclear-
power-stations-new-article/
[131] I don't know who gave permission, but it sure wasn't me.
[132] https://en.wikipedia.org/wiki/List_of_nuclear_weapons_tests
[133] When John D. Rockefeller was the richest man in the world, a reporter
asked him how much money would be enough. Rockefeller said, "Just a
little bit more." That is the answer of an addict, for whom there is never
"enough" of their drug of choice.
[134] I mean, Bangladesh is buying a nuclear reactor from Russia, and the
nuclear establishment has been relentless in their push to sell nuclear
technology to African nations. This is a move to permanent nuclear
enslavement, Cold War-type alliances being forged forever. See, there are
no aftermarket parts for nukes. If a country buys its nuclear reactor from
Russia, they are tied in to Russian nuclear technology, expertise, training,
and spare parts forever. If a country that has this technology tries to
politically oppose Russia in some meaningful way, Russia can simply
remove its personnel, not provide fresh fuel rods (they're not
interchangeable between models) and crucial replacement equipment,
Then that country is stranded with a decaying nuclear time bomb up close
and personal with their country, until and unless they succumb to the
Russian's will. Same goes if nukes are supplied by China or the U.S. Once
a country goes nuclear, it will always be indebted if not enslaved to the
nuclear power it bought from. Which goes a long way towards explaining
why: BANGLADESH! AFRICA! DON'T DO IT! DON'T GO NUCLEAR!!
[135] SEE: *Stand and Deliver*, the movie.
[136] https://www.youtube.com/watch?v=yfBWxw07h-E
[137] Well, maybe not richer than Jeff Bezos.
[138] With apologies to Rabbi Hillel, who wrote: "If I am not for myself, who
will be for me? If I am not for others, what am I? And if not now, when?"
[139] My favorite "alarmist" is Paul Revere. He raised the alarm. People
responded. It was a good thing.
[140] From "Suffer the Little Children" by Buffy Ste. Marie on the
Illuminations album (1969). www.amazon.com/Illuminations-Buffy-
Sainte-
Marie/dp/B001EWIZQ4/ref=sr_1_1?ie=UTF8&qid=1527191439&sr=8-
1&keywords=buffy+sainte+marie%2C+illuminations

TMI/40 – A Proposal

[141] I might even be enticed into performing *Aarmageddon*'s "Only One Mile from Three Mile Island" as Marlene Dietrich in *The Blue Angel*, or *KAZOO'S* "I'm Scared, Too" – the song I "downloaded" the morning after evacuation.

Afterword

[142] Remember that in the battle of David v. Goliath, David won.

Libbe HaLevy
Available Theatre Properties

PLAY SCRIPTS

NEW! *Marilyn: The Final Session* – Marilyn Monroe and a feminist therapist meet and clash in Purgatory. A play about women, abuse, and power. Two acts, 2W, unit set.

THE "CAROLYN" CYCLE

Shattered Secrets – Seven incest survivors, including Carolyn, join in a self-created "renegade" 12-Step-type meeting to share their pain and vent rage over their childhood sexual abuse… and this one night, things go out of control. Full length one-act, 4W/3M, minimal unit set. Internationally produced, award-winning, ran 2-1/2 years in Los Angeles.

Pearls that Coalesce – Three aspects of a single woman (Carolyn) wage war inside her psyche as she struggles to accept her sexuality. One act, 3W, bare stage.

Thanksgiving – Carolyn returns home for her family's annual dysfunctional get-together to confront them with the truth about her childhood. The problem: she has changed but they have not. Two acts, 5W/2M, unit set. Winner, National Gay Playwriting Award.

Sexual Sushi – Carolyn, in a happy lesbian relationship, starts an affair with a married man. Two acts, 2W/3M, unit set.

MUSICALS

KAZOO: A Musical Myth – A dysfunctional family spends the day in KAZOO, an amusement park where all the rides are emotional confrontations, never suspecting that if they stay in the park past sundown, they will be trapped inside forever. **The Three Mile Island musical.** 3W/3M/Chorus of 4W/3M. Award-winning libretto and lyrics complete; seeking professional composer w/the musical skills, work ethic, and equipment to create a modern, quality demo.

AARMAGEDDON: The Living End! – An adolescent girl gets stuck in a virtual reality computer programmed with all the worst fears of her aging-hippie father. A positive look at the end of the world. 2/3 written and composed; seeking composer/partner and/or submissions of Broadway-level satiric scenes and songs to complete. Query before submission.

For further information, contact:
Libbe HaLevy
LibrettoDoc@gmail.com

Learn Best Possible Ways to Protect Against Nuclear Radiation:

Radiation Awareness Protection Talk (RAPT)

*Created by **Nuclear Hotseat's Libbe HaLevy** and **Certified Nutrition Educator Kimberly Roberson, Founder, Fukushima Fallout Awareness Network...***

DID YOU KNOW?

- **Exposure to even so-called "low level" nuclear radiation,** is proven to **increase your risks of cancer, heart attacks, immune system diseases, miscarriages** and **birth defects.**
- **Fukushima** continues to contaminate the Pacific Ocean **every day** with **thousands of tons of highly radioactive water.**
- *All* nuclear reactors release harmful radiation into the environment.
- In the United States, **there is NO ongoing testing of our food, air or water** to determine the **radiation risks** we face.

RAPT: Information Is Power

With the RAPT Program, you will learn:
- **Foods** to avoid as likely to be **contaminated** by radiation.
- **Foods to eat** that help **boost your immune system** and **help resist radiation damage.**
- How to **detoxify your body** from **radiation exposure.**
- Best ways to **minimize radiation** in **your home water, air.**
- **Supplements to take** – including those **given to children after Chernobyl** – proven to **lessen the amount of radiation** in the body.

Nuclear Hotseat
Nuclear News... from a Different Perspective
www.*NuclearHotseat*.com

Every week, *Nuclear Hotseat* brings you News, In-depth Interviews, Activist Shout-Outs, "Numnutz of the Week" for Nuclear Boneheadedness, delivered with Producer/Host Libbe HaLevy's inimitable sense of humor and absurdity.

Interviews have included:
- Japanese Prime Minister Naoto Kan and Japanese Ambassador to Switzerland Mitsuhei Murata
- Award-winning investigative journalists Greg Palast, Karl Grossman, Susannah Frame
- Hollywood's Ed Asner, Ed Begley, Jr., Esai Morales
- Engineers, scientists, doctors, authors, researchers, epidemiologists, politicians, activists, and victims of the nuclear industry in the U.S., Japan, India, Australia, New Zealand, UK, Ireland, Brazil, Italy, Germany, Canada, Marshall Islands, South Africa., and more.

Nuclear Hotseat's Reach is Global:
- Downloaded in 123 countries on six continents
- Half a million downloads on a single episode
- In continuous weekly production since June, 2011
- Syndicated for a growing network of Broadcast stations by the Pacifica Audioport Network

Available for Upload, Download, Posting, Syndication

Get free email notification of each week's episode at: *NuclearHotseat*.com, scroll down to Yellow sign-up box.

Nuclear Hotseat... It's da bomb!

Book as Your Next Speaker...

Libbe HaLevy
Producer/Host, Nuclear Hotseat

Knowledgeable Passionate Articulate Funny

If the love child of Edward R. Murrow & Lily Tomlin
were raised by Jon Stewart & Rachel Maddow
you'd have *Nuclear Hotseat*'s irreverent **Libbe HaLevy**.

Media Appearances on Nuclear and Other Issues:
- TEDxPasadena
- *60 Minutes*
- New York – WCBS-TV News
- Boston – *Sonya Hamlin Show*, WBZ-TV; *Catch 44*, WGBH/WGBX-TV; affiliates of ABC, CBS, NBC
- Los Angeles – TV news interviews on KTTV, KTLA, KCBS, KNBC; Lila Garrett's *Connect the Dots*, KPFK-FM
- Featured Guest: *Coast-to-Coast AM* with George Noory; Art Bell's *Midnight in the Desert* with both Heather Wade and Dave Schrader; Michael Ruppert's *The Lifeboat Hour*

Topics Include:
- Making the Invisible Visible: Your Local Neighborhood Nuclear Radiation Risks (and you've got 'em!)
- Radiation Health Protection: Best Possible Practices
- Women, Radiation, Fertility, and DNA
- How to Ban the Bomb with your Bank Account
- **Individualized topics based on region and concerns.**

**To book Libbe HaLevy as a Speaker, Workshop Leader,
or Guest for TV/Radio/Online Media:**

Send an email to: YesIGlowintheDark@gmail.com

Like this book?
Give it a 5 and a 2!

On Amazon,
give it a 5-star review.
This will help with my
visibility online.

Then tell 2 friends about it.
Let's make it like the ping
pong balls on the mousetraps:
build to a genuine "nuclear
reaction" of a different sort.

Thank you!

Made in United States
North Haven, CT
08 May 2022

19030447R00133